Dress
Code

Dress Code

Understanding the Hidden Meanings
of Women's Clothes

BY TOBY FISCHER-MIRKIN

Clarkson Potter/Publishers
New York

Published by Clarkson Potter/Publishers, 201 East 50th Street, New York, New York 10022. Member of the Crown Publishing Group.

Random House, Inc. New York, Toronto, London, Sydney, Auckland

CLARKSON N. POTTER, POTTER, and colophon are trademarks of Clarkson N. Potter, Inc.

Manufactured in the United States of America

Design by Paula R. Szafranski

Library of Congress Cataloging-in-Publication Data

Fischer-Mirkin, Toby.
Dress code : Understanding the hidden meanings of women's clothes
/ by Toby Fischer-Mirkin.—1st ed.
p.   cm.
Includes index.
1. Clothing and dress—Psychological aspects.   2. Fashion—
Psychological aspects.   I. Title.
GT524.F55 1995   94-44839
391´.2´019—dc20   CIP

ISBN 0-517-59329-7

10 9 8 7 6 5 4 3 2 1

First Edition

This book is dedicated to my
beloved grandparents

Acknowledgments are warmly granted to:

Meredith Bernstein, who is the best friend and agent a writer can have.

Geraldine Stutz for her brilliant vision and for making me realize that angels come in the form of kindred spirits.

My editor, Pam Krauss, who through her graceful editing turned this into the best book it could possibly be.

Laura Golden Bellotto for her compassion and editorial advice.

Mitchell Mirkin for his encouragement and support.

Jonathan Edwards for his love.

To my family, Elaine, David, Cary, and Mitchell Fischer.

Shauna Scoll for her endless trips to the F.I.T. Library.

To the talented zeitgeists in the fashion industry who lent me their knowledge—Bill Blass, Michael Gross, Valentino, Oscar de la Renta, Eleanor Lambert, Paloma Picasso, Valentino, Isaac Mizrahi,

Sonia Rykiel, Donatella and Gianni Versace, Mary McFadden, Zandra Rhodes, Richard Blackwell, Louis Dell Olio, Fred Hayman, the late Giorgio Sant Angelo, the late Tina Chow, Louis Licari, Margaret Walch, Betsey Johnson, and Elin Saltzman.

To the many brilliant psychologists and psychoanalysts who help shed light on some very important issues—Dr. Helen De Rosis, Dr. Rita Freedman, Dr. Joan Lange, Dr. Michael Cunningham, Dr. Ann Kearney Cooke, Dr. Alathena Horner, Dr. Stephanie Geller, Dr. Alexandra Symonds, Dr. Dorian Leib, Sandy Klein, Dr. Dino Zanini.

Nancy and Lynn Ferrari—my original godmothers of this book.

Special thanks to Gladys Perint Palmer for her exquisite illustrations.

And to the friends and colleagues who encouraged me along the way—Katina Alexander, Judy Rothman, Blake and Kaitlin O'Leary, Sheila Grossman, Harold Stone, Denis Hand, Felicia Halpren, Anne Tamsberg, and Elizabeth Cavanaugh at the Meredith Bernstein Agency.

Contents

Introduction

*"Clothing is lifeless, without strength, it is an object.
Woman uses this object as a representation. It symbolizes
the impression that a woman wants to give of herself, but
it's her body that plays. That body which will make her
mysterious, strange, or seductive."*

—Sonia Rykiel

It is the spring of 1980, at the end of a day on which I have covered
three designers' fall collections. I am standing in an elevator on my
way to yet another show. Tired as I am, I can't help but notice the
extravagantly attired woman directly across from me. She is dressed
in the height of chic, adorned with elegant accessories, her hair perfectly coiffed, her makeup impeccable. Yet there is something
unnerving about this woman's appearance. Beneath her fashionable
facade she appears fragile, like someone carefully shielding herself
from the outside world. Suddenly I am possessed by the urge to walk
over to her, to see if she's okay. When the elevator stops, I reach
out to touch her arm, only to realize that what I have touched is a
mirror. The woman is me.

That jolting experience fifteen years ago was a revelation. It
made me realize how our clothing and appearance have the ability to
reveal things about us that we may not be aware of or cannot express
verbally. We are often so unconscious of the image we project that,
like me facing myself in that mirrored elevator, our own public persona becomes almost unrecognizable.

1

INTRODUCTION

In an attempt to answer the questions that have fascinated me since my "elevator awakening"—questions concerning the hidden messages we send through the clothing we choose to wear—I have spent the last five years interviewing psychologists, fashion analysts, art curators, and social researchers about how fashion has evolved and how it reflects outwardly our internal desires and conflicts. In the course of my research I discovered that numerous and complex motives inform our clothing decisions and that our personal style can be a strong reflection of our sense of self. *Dress Code* grew out of this research and my desire to reveal the psychology behind a woman's clothing choices in order to help women understand what their clothes are saying to others and how they can use this information to better understand themselves.

In revealing the psychological implications of appearance, *Dress Code* affords you the opportunity to consider more deeply what your clothes convey about who you are. You'll find out what it means when women dress to shock; how our sexual attitudes are reflected in the cut of our dress, the shape of our shoes, or the length of our hair; why some women are attracted to adolescent, masculine, or ethnic styles; how "appearance perfectionists" may be trying to cover up something about themselves; why wearing a full skirt in a business setting elicits a more trusting response than a fitted one; what it is we're drawn to in a particular clothing texture, color, or shape—and what those elements convey when we wear them.

While this is not intended as a hard-and-fast fashion guide—only you can know how much of your persona you care to reveal or how you want to be perceived by friends, colleagues, or others in your world—*Dress Code* will help you understand the meaning of your fashion choices and provide you with the tools for honing the image you want to present to others.

In the process, you may recognize how your attitudes toward various styles have been shaped and learn how to resolve discrepancies between your "look" and your inner self.

There's much more to style than fashion magazines would have us believe. The garments with which we cover our bodies every day are encoded with fascinating but usually unexplored meanings. I invite you to explore fashion on a deeper level. In so doing, you'll learn to unravel and decode those meanings and send the fashion signals that authentically reflect the real you.

The Power of Fashion

*"Clothes are never a frivolity: they always mean some-
thing, and that something is to a large extent outside the
control of our conscious minds."*
                                    —*James Laver,* Modesty in Dress

A woman stands before her closet, preparing for a night out.
She pulls out her favorite evening dress—a slinky black
one-shoulder knit gown. But soon she decides the clingy
fabric accentuates the few extra pounds she's put on and the black
drains the color from her face. Next she tries on the designer suit
she bought on sale, but she thinks perhaps the color is too bright for
that time of year. The strapless taffeta with the pouf looks dated, the
one-sleeved jacket too trendy. And so it goes for an hour, until, after
trying on a dozen "wrong" outfits, she turns to her husband, throws
up her hands, and wails, "I have nothing to wear!"

In all likelihood her husband would be puzzled that a woman
with piles of clothing strewn on every surface in her bedroom can't
find a single suitable outfit. But what he doesn't realize is that his
wife's statement may have nothing to do with her clothes at all.
Rather, it has everything to do with the woman staring back at her in
the mirror, how she feels about that woman, what impression she
wants to make in the evening ahead.

The act of deciding what to wear on any given day has repercussions that go far beyond simply reaching into the closet and putting together an outfit. You may love the act of dressing or you may dread it, but whether your selections are made out of impulse or calculation, your choices are *always* profoundly revealing—whether you know it or not.

Close your eyes and conjure up an image of the ideal you; now mentally reach into that woman's closet and pull out three outfits: one for a party or formal occasion, another for a business meeting, and a third for a casual afternoon spent running errands or shopping. Have this hypothetical woman spare no expense in assembling her wardrobe.

Now evaluate your choices. Let's say for the business meeting you imagined your ideal self wearing a tailored slim dark skirt, a classic buttoned-down white shirt, a blazer cinched with a wide belt, and pumps, creating a look that is urbane yet conservative. For the party you envisioned a short, body-hugging dress in a sensual fabric and high heels. In such an outfit you would feel alluring and receptive. For casual wear your ideal outfit is dark leggings or jeans and a black sweater, a combination you consider casual yet sophisticated. What do these choices say about who you are and how you want others to see you? Do these fashion choices project the same image you have in your mind's eye?

You may have thought, for example, that by wearing a sexy, revealing dress and high heels, you were expressing the seductive side of your personality. In fact, the dress is likely to cause others to see you as powerless and vulnerable because so much of your body is exposed and because the heels and snug dress do not allow you to move comfortably. In your tailored business outfit you may feel confident and pulled together, but your colleagues may perceive you as overly controlled and remote.

Your leggings and a sweater may make you feel comfortable and relaxed, but others would not respond to you as openly in that somber outfit as they would have if you had chosen brighter, warmer colors.

All clothing sends out messages about its wearer, some we intend and others we do not. A woman who enjoys antique lace dresses, old floral prints, and silky crocheted sweaters may assume she is giving off an air of fragile femininity. Those she encounters, however, may interpret this look to mean that she's extremely passive. The woman who dresses down for all occasions may feel she has nothing to prove and would rather dazzle with her intellect than with her attire, but others may consider her lack of effort to be a sign of disrespect.

Fashion is powerful. By understanding the clothes that work well for you in business and personal relationships, you can enhance both your private and professional life. Clothing can express your serious side, your sense of humor, your creativity, and your sexual nature. What you wear can both create a positive impression and make you feel good about yourself.

When you consider the time, effort, and money you spend on your appearance, you must admit that it plays an important part in your life. But you must put it in its rightful place. Fashion statements should never control you. Rather, you can learn to use your appearance and your clothing as tools of empowerment.

The purpose of *Dress Code* is to help you express who you really are through your various fashion choices and, just as important, to help you avoid giving unintended signals. Many times what we intend to express when we slip on a particular outfit is at odds with the image we do, in fact, project. When we communicate our identity visually, or miscommunicate it, those around us form misleading impressions about who we really are and respond to us accordingly—often to our consternation and utter bafflement.

Becoming aware of how others "read" our fashion language enables us to make clothing decisions based not only on what feels comfortable and seems pleasing to us, but on how we're being perceived by others.

The physical proportions, fabric, and style of our clothing does affect how others will react to us in rather reliable ways. Marilyn De Long and Ann Marie Fiore at the University of Minnesota explored how clothing conveys symbolic messages. Their study showed that subjects made a strong connection between sweater styles and the personality they attributed to the wearer.

Their findings suggested the following:

◆ A woman who wears a sweater that reaches to her hips and is made from a thin, supple knit is perceived as sophisticated and mature.

◆ A sweater in a bulky texture of hipbone length in a dark color with a pattern or a motif indicates someone who is easygoing and friendly.

◆ A deep V-neck sweater in a fine knit conveys a romantic, sensual personality.

◆ A sweater of medium bulkiness connotes an individual who is composed, logical, and efficient.

Although such correlations may seem simplistic, these findings do show that people readily form impressions based on very superficial fashion cues.

Consider another study conducted at Murdoch University in Australia, where Keith Gibbons and Jeffrey Conroy studied the impact of the physical dimensions of a woman's clothing and how these correspond to personality traits. They discovered that the length and width of a woman's skirt is a good indicator of her disposition:

- A woman who chooses a long, slim skirt tends to be more sophisticated and intellectual, but less open emotionally.

- One who wears a long, full skirt is usually very open and easygoing (in part because of the freedom of movement of the skirt), but not as sophisticated as the woman in a slimmer skirt.

- Short skirts suggest to the viewer a very youthful, open-minded, creative person.

- Short pleated skirts that swing point to a more carefree nature.

Overall, as the length and fullness varied, so did the wearer's perceived level of sophistication. The wider the skirt, the more friendly the woman was judged to be.

The styling and fabric of our clothing communicate a great deal about our self-image. A woman wearing a low-cut, double-breasted jacket in a soft wool crepe appears more flexible than one in a double-breasted stiff wool gabardine jacket with six buttons. The buttons are a visible barrier between the woman and the outside world, making her seem standoffish or unapproachable.

All this is a way of saying there is enormous room for interpretation in the fashion zone. We may feel fashionable and sexy in our transparent décolletage bodysuit, but to men it may appear suggestive, to other women offensive or intimidating. When we sport our new ensemble, we may feel right in step with the latest fashion but may instead come across as haughty. Adopting the latest trend in street fashion may make us feel vibrant and energetic but might say to others that we're trying to deny the inevitability of aging.

"Good taste is simplicity. Bad taste is not understanding the purity of simplicity."—Mary McFadden

---

With all this going on, dressing appropriately no longer means hiding behind the safe facade of a cookie-cutter uniform or slavishly adhering to the latest fashion decrees. It means striking a balance, finding a mode of dress that is true to who you are yet ensures that signals aren't confused.

Clothing is a window into both a woman's conscious and unconscious being. Our clothing reveals volumes on how we feel about ourselves and offers a glimpse into our desires, our fantasies, and our values. The act of putting together an outfit also draws upon our artistic sensibility and our imagination. Our body is a canvas upon which we layer fabrics and color to create a pleasing self-portrait. In so doing, we express different dimensions of ourselves and decide how much to reveal about who we are.

A woman can also use clothing to enhance aspects of her personality that she feels are undeveloped. For example, if you need to bolster your self-confidence, you can zip yourself into a black leather motorcycle jacket, top it off with a jaunty leather cap, and shimmy into bicycle shorts adorned with silver chains to make others believe that you're tough and aggressive—at least for an evening.

If you're tired of looking like a responsible executive, you can transform yourself into a timeless romantic for an evening at home with your husband or lover. Through clothing you can get in touch with your emotions and sense of self. Putting together a look is a form of self-creation that can't be done and undone at will. But fashion needn't be—shouldn't be—a mere costume, a false image that cloaks who and what we really are. Each of us embodies a complexity of traits, proclivities, and tastes, and we have the option of exposing different facets of our characters according to the changing roles we play and the life circumstances in which we find ourselves. We may want to appear adventurous and provocative one day, mature and conservative the next, demure and dramatic the day after that. Still, each of these looks can honestly reflect who we are—if we know how to use fashion to our advantage.

The trick to successful dressing—not dressing for success, a tired, dated concept—lies in the details. How does a collar, a neck or hemline, a cut or drape, subtly change the entire aspect of our appearance? Even within the confines of a proper navy suit, a blouse or a shoulder pad can make the difference between a provocative, creative, or commanding impression. How do accessories like shoes, gloves, and hats alter the effect of an entire outfit? And how can we make the cultural associations of certain garments or styles (such as an equestrian-inspired jacket or a designer suit that speaks affluence) work in our favor? The following are examples of our everyday clothing choices and what they say about who we are and what we're feeling.

◆ Our clothes can confer status in the professional world. His-for-her fashion, man-tailored pantsuits, and the masculine look in general may make some of us feel stronger and more powerful. Knowing which collars, jackets, pants, and shirts signal authority and which denote powerlessness can provide us with a certain leverage in the workplace.

◆ At times we may choose to present an overtly sexual image.

DRESS CODE

Clothing that draws attention to body parts, such as push-up bras that make décolletage more alluring, backs that plunge to the cleavage of the derriere, clinging bodysuits, and poufs all send a clear message of sexual invitation. Clothing can contain potent sexual symbolism, from bustiers with breast cones to high-heeled shoes that thrust the body out of alignment, turning your walk into a sexy strut. Even a chaste ponytail becomes a sexual lure when twirled into a chignon that resembles an inverted phallic symbol.

"Our external image is our messenger, a public declaration. Certain disguises are strongly linked to our innermost fears and in these cases a dress acts as a shield to hide and protect us."—Gianni Versace

---

◆ There are times when we don't want to be seen—or when we don't want our true selves to show through—and clothing serves as the perfect cover. Clothing can provide camouflage, from a simple scarf and sunglasses donned for a trip to the grocery store to the professional "costumes" we wear when presenting ourselves for a job interview.

◆ Clothing can provide protection—not only from the elements but from whatever looms on the psychological landscape. When we're in a hostile or unknown environment, we may find ourselves instinctively wrapping ourselves up, buttoning our jacket, or tightening the belt around our coat. Certain pieces of clothing—often old and well worn—have warm associations that bestow on the wearer a sense of comfort that trendier articles cannot.

◆ When the pressures of contemporary life threaten to over-

whelm, fashion can provide an escape to another time, another way of life, in just the time it takes to slip into a vintage flowered dress or a towering pair of platform wedges. Donning the clothing of an earlier era is one way many of us express our longing for a time when life was not so decadent, rushed, and impersonal as it sometimes seems today.

In all of these ways and countless others, fashion can contribute to our overall sense of security and well-being.

Clothing can also give a subtle boost to a woman's self-esteem. The pervasive media images of the "ideal" woman conspire against all but the most self-assured of us to undermine our body confidence. This is partly why so many of us are uncertain about the clothing, hairstyle, and makeup choices we make. Women often experience tremendous anxiety over our efforts to perfect our outward appearance. We learn from an early age that how we look and what we wear enables us to "fit in"; the wrong choices can reveal the chinks in our armor.

It often takes years to undo negative feelings about our bodies. The woman who was overweight as a child may still hide behind baggy clothes, even though she is now toned and lithe. The tall woman who always felt ungainly may deliberately choose nondescript styles rather than accentuate her exotic look or dramatic height. And the petite, curvaceous woman may wear heels and dresses designed for a taller woman while hiding her voluptuous curves.

We all need to dress in harmony with our body. Rather than buy into society's admonishments that we're less than ideal, we need to acknowledge who we are and work with what we have. And it is just as important for each of us to distinguish between who we are and the fantasy of who we wish we were.

THE ROLE OF TASTE

"Taste. Where does it come from? Good taste, besides being inwardly clear, has to be outwardly fit".

—*Santayana*

At any point in the cycle of fashion, designers and retailers offer a wide spectrum of options from which to choose. Personal taste will play a large role in how you make these choices. Developing good taste means learning how to reconcile what attracts you with what is appropriate for your body type, your age, and the occasion.

Taste affects the way we coordinate clothing and blend colors, patterns, and fabrics. A woman with "taste" can strike a balance that feels harmonious to her and looks appropriate to those around her. She is in step with fashion yet not enslaved by it, incorporating new looks and proportions while giving them her own stamp. Some women are simply born with a sense of color and design; they can accurately assess color, lines, and styles and know which will work for them and which will not just by looking in the mirror. But training and experience can enhance any woman's ability to achieve an effect that is fashionable.

Knowing when a garment is suited to the occasion is an element of being tasteful. Wearing a cocktail dress, no matter how elegant, to a barbecue is in bad taste. We can all learn a lot by trial and error and by being honest enough to learn from our mistakes.

Outside influences affect one's taste as well. Exposing yourself to music and art and the world around you enables you to develop a sense of what is inherently beautiful. This sensibility will naturally assert itself when you get dressed each morning.

Your parents' aesthetic also has a bearing upon your taste. How they dressed and decorated their home is a part of who you were— and are. My grandmother was extremely creative and put clothes together with a distinctive flair. I grew up under the influence of a very positive example. Are there people in your life who serve as fashion role models? Is it because they have that uncanny ability to "be themselves" while incorporating the best of contemporary trends?

Fortunately, good taste is something you can develop and refine by understanding yourself, your body, your face, and what suits you. Learning to stress your strongest physical assets and knowing how to deemphasize problem areas is a part of good taste, as is using color to complement your eyes, skin tone, and hair and choosing lines that flatter your figure. Understanding how differences in form and fabric affect how you look is also important.

Once you learn these basic elements, taste will become instinctive. We can cultivate a fashion instinct by sharpening our awareness

of color, shape, and fabric in much the same way we appreciate any other art form. Once we know how rhythm, tone, and melody fit together, we instinctively recognize a great song . . . and find ourselves tapping our feet and humming along. And once you discover a style of dressing that both complements your physical attributes and expresses your creativity, you will feel more comfortable and confident in your clothes.

DISCOVERING YOUR OWN STYLE

It is only natural to want to be as stylish and attractive as possible. Fortunately, few women still live up to the cookie-cutter ideals of beauty as defined by society. We are learning to be comfortable with ourselves as real women—with unique qualities and interesting and acceptable imperfections. It's wonderful to see a woman whose outer appearance truly reflects her inner self. And at long last, the fashion industry is learning to look to women for inspiration, not the other way around.

By understanding your own subtle, often unconscious motivations for dressing the way you do, you'll discover which stylistic elements you want to retain, which you want to enhance, and which you want to change. As you read this book, you'll begin to shape your own fashion persona from the myriad design, fabric, texture, and color alternatives available to you. Whether you're wondering if that red ruffled dress looks more silly or exotic or if those clunky, square-toed shoes are really, truly you, with a confident sense of your own personal style, you'll be able to make the fashion choices that honestly—and beautifully—reflect who you are.

Communicating with Color

"All colors are the friends of their neighbors and the lovers of their opposites."

—*Chazel*

Color is perhaps the most potent force in fashion communication. Within seconds of meeting you, others will respond to the "color messages" flashed by your clothing. Color can influence the viewer's hormones, blood pressure, and body temperature. It has the power to stimulate or depress, invite or repel. Thus, before we dress for a particular occasion, we must consciously consider not only how colors make us, the wearers, feel and what they communicate about our personalities but how others react unconsciously when they view the colors we wear.

In general, your color preferences reveal to others whether you tend to focus inward or outward. Knowing this, you can choose those colors that will bring you the kind of attention you desire and turn a social situation to your advantage. For example, since dark colors like black or navy recede, wearing them allows you to keep a low profile; bold, bright colors such as turquoise or yellow create an expectation of warmth and gregariousness. On the other hand, the woman in black, introverted as she might appear, is also viewed as more sophisticated than her counterpart in a vivid pink suit.

PALETTE OF EMOTIONS:
HOW COLOR AFFECTS OUR MOODS

Not knowing quite why, we find ourselves repeatedly choosing particular items of clothing in our closet at certain times in our life, strongly attracted to the color for some distinct reason. Haven't we all had the experience of reaching instinctively for a fire engine–red blazer, a creamy white blouse, a pale blue sweater, knowing on some level we were emotionally "in sync" with that color at that moment? Some colors enhance the wearer's creativity, some make her feel more sensuous, others improve her business performance. Sometimes without even realizing it, we rely on color to bring us pleasure, power, or sexual attention.

Each of us reacts differently to specific colors, based in part on our environment, upbringing, and culture. We may have been told as a child that we looked ghastly in red. In fact, we may look wonderful in red, but our early negative experience makes us continue to feel uncomfortable wearing it. Also, color that serves as a magnet to some people may act as a repellent to others. One person may see red and think passion, while another connects red to aggression.

"Living without colors is senseless and absurd for they illuminate, revive, lift up, and bring pleasure to those who wear them and to those who look at them."—Gianni Versace

Every color has certain cultural connotations as well. For instance, in the Asian culture, red is used for wedding dresses, since it is not only believed to ward off demons but was worn as the color of royalty and aristocracy during the Middle Ages. In our society, however, red represents blood, rage, and danger—but it also symbolizes eroticism and passion.

For some, yellow may represent sunshine; to others, decay. If you identify with the expression *green with envy*, you might have a negative reaction to green, but if you cherish your time out in nature, green may represent beauty and the environment. If your best friend's ex-husband had a penchant for navy, that color may be repulsive to her, whereas your love for nautical activities might endow it with strong positive associations.

Our choice of color goes beyond mere "taste." Whether color associations are learned or ingrained, our preferences can reveal much about our experience and personality. Wearing one color on a constant basis, for example, could reveal that we're experiencing difficult times or looking for stability. A case in point was an attorney who left the legal profession after fifteen years and took a year off to recoup. During this time, she found herself constantly wearing white. The color of summer vacations and a clean slate, white is neutral and symbolizes surrender. It was a color that didn't expect anything of her, allowing her to stay in her own space.

Another woman who had spent half her life rebelling against her mother found that the colors she had always stayed away from, red and gold, were two of her mom's favorites. Only after she resolved the issues with her mother could the woman reintegrate red and gold into her wardrobe.

Color can stimulate or tranquilize. A study done at the Wagner Institute of Color found that when spending time in the presence of someone wearing a cool-colored suit, such as green or blue, we may feel as though time has slowed. Yet spending time with someone dressed in yellow or red will make us feel time is moving quickly. Some colors infuse us with life while others cause us to be introspective. If, for instance, we're feeling tired or irritable, light shades of green can heal and rejuvenate us, while slipping into something pink can ease our anxiety or frustration. Bright, warm colors in soft fabrics such as cotton or cashmere can help us radiate cheerfulness, uplifting the mood of those in our presence.

HARNESSING COLOR'S POWER

We all subconsciously use color to convey our moods, personality, and insecurities. Each of us responds to color differently based on our emotional makeup, but certain colors have universal associations. We need not leave our color choices solely to the subconscious. We can actively choose colors appropriate to a given situation or goal or to heighten or disguise our emotional outlook.

Color can lend status, make a statement, or influence others. It can stimulate, inspire, or calm; create an image of power, sophistication, openness, or intellectuality. A woman must know which tones work well in a given context and which will work against her. Knowing how to use color to your best advantage is definitely an art in itself.

COLOR COMBINING

Understanding how to mix colors is essential to creating an effect that is both pleasing and harmonious. To get ideas, look for color schemes you find attractive not only in fashion spreads and ads in magazines, but in fine art, paintings, and nature.

Learning to combine various shades correctly and avoid those that don't mix well is part of using color to its fullest power. Start with a basic like black, red, beige, navy, or white and then add splashes of your favorite color. Black, for instance, looks great with shocking pink, peach, lemon yellow, or pale blue. Shades of beige look wonderful with red or peach. Navy is elegant accented with red or pink. Wearing a red wrap with a navy suit and classic white shirt adds an uplifting color, as does throwing a shocking pink scarf across a black suit. Beige is a combination of white and brown, so choosing brown or white accents or combinations would look flattering.

Complementary Color Chart:
How to Mix Neutrals with Color

With Black, Camel, Gray,
or Tweed

Bright colors to energize and
warm up your outfit:
SHOCKING PINK
FUCHSIA
RED
YELLOW RED
ORANGE
TURQUOISE

Pastels to soften the starkness
of neutral colors:
LILAC

23

DRESS CODE

PALE YELLOW
BABY BLUE
PALE GREEN
PEACH
PINK

Colors that add another
dimension:
SILVER
GOLD

Rich colors:
BURGUNDY, WINE, PLUM
HUNTER GREEN
EMERALD GREEN
RUST
PUMPKIN

Whites and off-whites for
contrast and to soften:
CREAM
IVORY
WHITE

With Navy

Light colors that contrast
nicely:
PALE PINK
PALE BLUE
PALE GREEN

For the classic look:
WHITE
RED

For a more vibrant look:
YELLOW
FUCHSIA
ORANGE

For a subtle contrast:
PURPLE

With Brown

To enrich:
RED
RED ORANGE
LIGHT ORANGE

To brighten and enliven:
YELLOW
CORAL
PINK

For a clean contrast:
WHITE
CREAM
IVORY

Some Examples of Strikingly
Good Color Combo Outfits

◆ A gray suit with a red cashmere sweater and silver accessories projects a sophistication infused with warmth and energy.

◆ Accents of camel or beige soften the formality of a black dress.

◆ A navy suit with yellow accents is businesslike yet cheerful.

◆ A fuchsia blouse offsets the seriousness of the navy suit it's paired with and makes it more fashionable.

◆ A white silk blouse underneath a purple suit or jacket combines the purity of the former and spirituality of the latter.

◆ Adding a touch of red to the subtlety and luxuriousness of a tan, cream, beige, or gold outfit will lend a spark of high emotion.

◆ Black with accents of orange sends a fun message.

◆ Black trousers, a black turtleneck, and boots in concert with a multicolored tweed jacket makes for an artistic look.

◆ A pale pink or plum scarf thrown over a charcoal-gray jumpsuit (and enhanced with silver accessories) sends a feminine and cerebral message.

◆ Soften the tough image of a black leather jacket by wearing a pastel sweater underneath it.

COLORS OF THE TIME

One need only look at back issues of fashion magazines to realize that contemporary culture, economy, and social concerns influence the national palette. The 1960s, an era of freedom and experimentation, was an exceptionally colorful time. Psychedelic colors flooded Carnaby Street in England. Designer Zandra Rhodes used neon orange, bright yellows, lush reds, and Indian pinks.

In contrast, the 1980s, clearly a decade of conservatism and prosperity, gave us black and "Nancy Reagan" red. Red and black, the colors of sex and power, flashed boldly down the runways in keeping with the prospering economy.

Among others, designers Donna Karan and Rei Kawakubo spun a multitude of their designs out of black. And Christian Lacroix offered the excessive fantasies of the eighties with his collages of bright, whimsical, rich colors.

According to Margaret Walch, director of the Color Association of America, fluctuations in color preferences are in direct relationship to the economy and the national mood. "Usually it reflects the economy. In a very good economy you will find bright, clean, clear colors. In a very poor economy, there will be what are called 'Depression-era colors.' The leaders, of course, are black and brown—followed by other dark, serious shades such as gray, burgundy, and grape."

COLORS OF THE SOUL

RAGING RED

Our fondness for red is linked to its properties as a stimulant. Red can increase body temperature and set off a hormonal chain reaction, including rapid heartbeat and quickened breath. It is also an erotically potent color, and the subtle differences in shade can affect the type of attention you attract. Deeper blue reds connote energy, warmth, talent, and courage. The deeper and more muted the red, the less sexually overwhelming it is. Such shades may be less striking, but they still radiate passion and sexual energy.

The specific shade of red influences the specific message it sends. A woman wearing a yellow-based red (such as tomato red) probably will attract more male attention than the woman wearing blue red. Yellow- or orange-based reds are more intense and arousing. Men are inherently attracted to the implicit "danger" of a yellow-based red. Bright red lips, for example, are a prime object of desire for men. In the 1920s, a time of growing freedom for the female sex, women painted their mouths into shocking red pouts to express their newly liberated sexuality. Marilyn Monroe's bright, lush mouth threw men into shivers of carnal lust, whereas Grace Kelly's pinkish red lips, symbolizing class and refinement, elicited reverence for her quiet beauty.

How do men's and women's responses to red differ? While yellow-based reds draw men's attention, women favor blue-based shades. A color response report published by Carlton Wagner of the Wagner Institute of Color in Santa Barbara, California, showed that males responded most strongly to midrange yellow-based reds, true primary reds, red wines, and matador red. Darker reds, pinks, and burgundies particularly appealed to upper-class men, who tended to be more experienced in business and more sophisticated psychologically. Women preferred burgundy red, plum, dark blue-based reds, and dark raspberry.

Women in red are often seen as flirtatious, dynamic, and playful. But red is also the color of dominance. A woman sheathed in a red dress says, "Look at me! I am in charge. I go after what I want. I quest. I conquer. I never settle for second best." In the movie *Working Girl,* Sigourney Weaver's character asserts her power with red when she marches dramatically into a room of blue-suited men, proclaiming her self-confidence and take-charge attitude. A striking example of red as the color of power and courage was its use in military uniforms. Red camouflaged bloodstains and made armies look more threatening. Blue-based reds reek of leadership and authority and are therefore a good choice for business situations. Red is a great color for commanding attention, recognition, or power.

Wearing red requires self-assurance and confidence and should be saved for special occasions or when you want to make a bold statement. In some instances, red is the worst color a woman can wear because it demands *too much* attention. It can be overly aggressive and intimidating and may set the scene for an uneasy interaction. For this reason, it is *not* the best choice for a first meeting or job interview.

Texture plays as important a role in tempering the effect of red as does hue. For example, cashmere, silk, or satin take the edge off vibrant reds; such fabrics create a softness that counterbalances the color's potency and are perfect for a romantic evening. Red leather, on the other hand, will always appear tough and brash, and red wool verges on harshness, emphasizing the color's association with power and aggression. In the deep tones, red velvet conveys richness. A woman wearing burgundy or crimson velvet will come across as both opulent and romantic. However, bright red velvet seems vulgar. Wearing a bodysuit of red lace is an overt appeal for sexual attention, and only those who want to attract it should wear one.

Since red is an intense color, you might need to temper your message. For instance, a red blazer inherently projects an intensity that can be softened with a white or black top underneath: adding black imbues the outfit with more sophistication, adding white softens the effect. Fashion-conscious pairing, such as a pink dress with a wonderful red shawl, could add a touch of confidence; it shows you are unafraid to experiment with color.

Red may be the most direct color message you can send. There are no hidden meanings here: passion and potency are directly communicated.

PLAYFUL PINK

In *Funny Face,* the classic Audrey Hepburn/Fred Astaire movie, a fashion editor disgruntled with the lackluster quality of her magazine's latest issue gets an inspiration when she eyes a bolt of pink fabric. "Think pink!" she exclaims excitedly to her staff. "Banish the black! Bury the beige! Red is dead! Blue is through!" she cries as she makes plans to spice up the magazine's next issue with an all pink spread.

Designer Elsa Schiaparelli introduced shocking pink to the fashion world in the 1930s, taking the ultrasweetness out of a color usually associated with baby girls and proclaiming the shocking version of the shade a hot fashion color. Regardless of the particular gradation, pink has positive connotations. Even the slang associated with pink is very upbeat: "tickled pink," meaning delighted; "in the pink," a state of good health.

Pink is red stripped of its anger and eroticism, but not its sensuality. It is a nurturing color, romantic and feminine. Pink is the color of tongues, flesh, and nipples. Pink's calming, nurturing essence encourages creativity. And pink also symbolizes our intuition.

Alexander Schauss, director of biological research at Washington University in Tacoma, Washington, studied the effects of pink on angry and frustrated individuals. He discovered that pink surroundings calm and soothe. A number of additional studies have confirmed Schauss's findings as well as shown the positive influence pink can have on creative pursuits.

Wearing pale or warm pink clothing puts others at ease. Since pink has a calming effect, wearing it sends signals that you're a gentle, caring person. Pink also carries a sense of youthful vitality.

Soft, yellow- and blue-based pinks are very affectionate and playful colors. These are the colors of children's birthday parties, colors that originate in fantasies. Shocking pinks and blue-based pinks are strong fashion colors that usually elicit positive responses from women, so they're good colors to wear when conducting a business meeting with other women. On the other hand, if you're trying to get closer to the man in your life, keep in mind that men find yellow-based pinks—such as peach, tangerine pink, and brownish pinks—very romantic.

BASIC BLACK

When a woman pulls her dependable "little black dress" from the closet, in all likelihood she is counting on the innate elegance of black, not to mention its ability to hide a few extra pounds. But on a less conscious level, mystery, prestige, and a tinge of rebellion may also be influencing her decision to shimmy into the black velvet dress, black power suit, or black leggings.

Black silhouettes the body, throwing light and shadow on a woman's curves. It lends a sense of drama to the features and can mask her flaws, make her look slimmer, set off a fair complexion. A woman garbed in black appears both intriguing and elegant. Depending upon the particular garment, black can also render its wearer invisible, stark, and severe. Adding touches of color can soften or enliven black's severity.

The lure of black is no secret. It is, hands down, the most chic color—invariably tasteful and appropriate when we're not sure what to wear. A subtle element of fear also contributes to black's erotic, sexual appeal. Darkness signifies the unknown and the complex. Prior to the current feminist sensibility, black was worn only by women perceived as sexually experienced.

One of the naughtiest hues when used in such garments as lace stockings or slip dresses, black has always been linked with erotica. And its association with the occult lends an ominous, forbidden quality to its allure. Black is perhaps at its most erotic in the form of a leather miniskirt, body-hugging ribbed turtleneck, trousers, or a lace bodysuit. It's at its most sophisticated in the form of black cashmere sweaters or the classic "little black dress." Black can also be extremely prim, as in the Pilgrim's dress or nun's habit. Religious orders and people in authority—priests, nuns, and police officers—also traditionally wear black.

Because black represents domination, a black suit remains the ultimate in power dressing and is favored by many women in positions of authority. (However, black may be *too* potent for middle management, since they haven't quite established themselves as leaders and may be perceived as looking overly authoritative.)

The archives of fashion are a testament to the clout of black. Designer Cristobal Balenciaga designed exclusively in black. In fact, black dominated the Spanish aesthetic as far back as the 1500s, when Spain's leaders all dressed in black. This is readily apparent in Diego Velásquez's paintings of Philip I, which portray him in opulent black fabrics with gold and silver trim.

Coco Chanel launched her "little black dress" in the 1920s. Since then, these versatile garments have come to be considered a universal passport to any event. In a black dress one need never worry about being under- or overdressed. A simple black dress can be worn every day with different accessories and always be fashionably correct.

Artists have traditionally favored black because it doesn't distract them from their work. Artistic women are drawn to black, as it allows them to reach into their dark side, to access the source of their best work.

Some of black's power may also come from its association with germination. All that is profound comes out of darkness, life from beneath the soil or the cloak of the womb. One can view black as a veneer for light. It is a creative color that waits for illumination to seep out from its darkness.

In the sixteenth century, Anne of Brittany originated the custom of wearing black for mourning. Her somber attire endowed her with an air of tragedy as well as mystery, and to this day black is still the color of mourning. In many countries widowed women wear black for the rest of their lives.

Black is also associated with evil, danger, and rebellion. In Jungian philosophy black represents the descent into hell and is connected with the dark and hidden subconscious. Black leather is a particularly rebellious combination of color and fabric that conjures up the image of 1950s rabble-rousers James Dean and Marlon Brando and, more recently, U2's Bono.

PURE WHITE

When we think of white, we think purity, innocence, and femininity. White has a virginal appeal in that it is the symbol of surrender. White is the color of the milk a woman produces to feed her babies. It is also the color of semen. White is devoid of deception or darkness. It is untainted and clean. Its innocence and clarity inspires trust in others. And, of course, the traditional bride about to lose her virginity dresses in white. When a woman wears white, she subliminally emits both a reproductive message and the chaste quality of the fragile young bride. (Interestingly, the white wedding dress did not actually gain prominence until the 1920s. Before then, women got married in dresses or gowns in the color of their choice.)

The glamorous side of white was depicted by the ivory satin gowns and white fox furs worn by 1930s film star Jean Harlow. Her platinum-blond hair accentuated the all-white vision she embodied.

There is also an ethereal, angelic aspect to white, as evidenced in the numerous classical paintings depicting white-frocked angels performing their celestial tasks.

White is considered a status color as well. A woman wearing a pristine white suit conveys the message that she need not worry about ruining her clean white clothes with strenuous work or menial chores. In other words, only those with a leisurely lifestyle can afford the luxury of wearing white on a daily basis. In fact, before the advent of washing machines and dry cleaning, white was the ultimate symbol of status, suggesting a woman of means who had someone to tend to her garments and keep them clean.

White is the color of virtue and altruism. It conjures up images of the scientist unlocking the mysteries of the universe or of doctors and nurses tending to the sick. White is also a nonthreatening color, which is why white-coated medical professionals emanate a quality of trustworthiness.

White is the perfect choice when we don't want to make a color decision. It makes us feel clean, renewed, and open to change. For each of us, there are times when no other color but white will do.

TRUE BLUE

Blue is universally loved and held in high regard by most cultures. It is the color of trust, dependability, and respect. Sky blue garments signal wisdom, spirituality, and the afterlife.

According to the Wagner Institute of Color, in the presence of a sky blue outfit, the brain produces eleven tranquilizing hormones, which is why people feel more relaxed in the presence of cool blues. Wearing blue puts others at ease and allows interactions to go more smoothly. When we dress in blue we appear introspective and wise. Blue signifies breeding, social status, stability, dignity. Thus blue may be the best color for a business suit when you want to inspire confidence. (An interesting aside: The term *blue blood* originated in Spain, where Moorish aristocrats believed they had bluer veins than those with mixed ancestry!)

Marine blues, associated with deep oceans and expansive skies, lend their wearers a sense of depth and profundity. Royal or lapis blues are affirmative colors suggesting faith and goodwill. When we wear royal blue we are often perceived as being more considerate. Interestingly, the origin of the color and its symbols go back to A.D. 431, when artists depicted Mary, mother of Jesus, in lapis blue.

Solid blues, such as navy, are synonymous with tradition and are the first choice of bankers and lawyers (stroll through the aisles at Brooks Brothers if you need proof of this). If you're looking for individuality, however, you will not find it in this color.

Creative people are not particularly fond of dark blue, preferring lighter, more whimsical shades of blue. Pale blues, for example, inspire fantasy and foster playfulness. They are the colors of children and adolescents, as well as the best colors to wear when you want to elicit kindness or feel more serene.

While blue is not suitable for formal evening attire (an invitation will never read "blue tie only"), it definitely belongs to the physical world of work and recreation. Think of denim blue jeans, chambray shirts, and the "blue-collar worker."

Because navy is not as light as blue or as dark as black, it combines trustworthiness and seriousness. It lifts the darkness out of black. Thus when a woman wears dark or navy or royal blue, people tend to both respect and feel comfortable around her. For this reason navy is perfect for conferences and business meetings—especially in the more conservative professions.

In 1915 the U.S. Navy chose dark blue as the official color for its dress uniforms. During the 1970s, dark blue became associated with Republicans and conservatism. Navy is the color of the preppie culture, the "old boy" network, and often the police department. Because it symbolizes authority, navy blue commands respect. However, some may see a woman in navy blue not only as organized and conservative but as narrow and rigid as well.

A study conducted by the Pantone Institute showed that blue green is among the most popular of all colors and held in especially high esteem by the upper echelons of society. Dark blue green symbolizes prestige, financial success, and good breeding. Women have an inherent attraction to shades of aqua and turquoise. We feel at ease and open up in the presence of these fanciful colors. Men react negatively to deeper shades of turquoise and positively to lighter aqua, so keep this in mind when dressing for a date. Both are colors of caprice and originality, and the fashion industry depends on them for accents.

SUNNY YELLOW

Yellow, one of the primary colors, triggers the part of the brain associated with anxiety and thus causes us to become more alert. It is the first color of the spectrum registered by the brain and the one that most quickly catches our eye. No wonder it is the color of most traffic signs! When we wear yellow, it indicates a unique power—especially in the case of a yellow suit. A political reporter in need of a quote told me, "I wore a marigold jacket, and the senator answered my question first. He said it was the only way he would be able to concentrate on the other questions."

Yellow is a complex color. When a woman wears yellow, she

demands attention but may cause others to become uncomfortable, irritable, or anxious. In the presence of yellow, some people may become distracted and more prone to lose their patience.

A group of professional women who meet on a regular basis to plan fund-raising events were waiting for one last person to arrive. On this occasion, as was often the case, most of the women in the group were wearing black or navy suits. After waiting fifteen minutes for the last member, they decided to start the meeting without her. When the tardy committee member arrived ten minutes later, she was wearing a blinding canary yellow suit and was brimming with apologies. Within minutes an air of unrest settled over the room. One woman began to argue about the seating arrangement. Another began fidgeting and tugging at her stockings. Still another found herself pulling out her sunglasses and slipping them on. Afterward one of the women, wondering what had made the meeting so uncomfortable, speculated that there was something upsetting about the yellow suit. "After a tough day in court," she said, "I need a tranquilizer, not a stimulant." Perhaps the committee bickering would have occurred even without the influence of the canary yellow, but it certainly added to the stressful feelings among the more solemnly dressed members.

Without question, yellow is a stimulant. It prompts a surge in the adrenal glands, causing hormones to flow and the pulse to throb. Yellow can increase one's anxiety level and induce restlessness. Other negative associations may derive from the yellow armbands worn by Jews in Nazi Germany and during the Spanish Inquisition.

On the other hand, yellow is also optimistic and reassuring. It is the color of the slicker worn by the rescuer who emerges from a fire or other emergency. It is the color of the sun, the first light of day. The sun's warmth and energy is responsible for all of life, which may be why yellow often symbolizes optimism.

Yellow signifies illumination and depicts the light of the intellect. Confucius favored yellow, which led to its association with wisdom. Worn in muted or pale tones, it is the color of artistic and philosophical detachment. Sunny yellow speaks of hope, the future, and sagacity. And because yellow is ephemeral, it can also be the color of anticipation. The sun rises and sets. Yellow leaves of autumn turn brown and drop off the trees. And, of course, van Gogh's famous sunflower forever imprinted the gloriousness of yellow onto our collective cultural consciousness.

The ultimate yellow is gold. Gold on clothing is a sign of luxury and prestige. It is the color of money and enlightenment. Financial associations give gold its special prestige, but because it can also seem ostentatious, it should be saved for special occasions. Gold lends a radiant glow to most women's skin, imbuing them with a patina of richness. However, metallic gold in bags and clothing, if done in poor quality, cheapens its brilliance.

PURPLE PASSION

In her book *Men in Love*, Nancy Friday writes, "A man has a reverie of meeting a blond woman in a purple nightgown. He doesn't know why the colors are exciting; his unconscious does but doesn't bother to explain. The man only knows the blonder, the purplier, the more heated he grows. Soon he is inventing scenarios of bare breasted models hired to test new peroxide hair bleaches, supplied by a company that arbitrarily orders all contestants to wear purple underwear. If the plot seems silly, what does it matter? The erotic has its reasons that reason doesn't know."

The feverish reaction depicted in this scenario illustrates the potent effect of color. Friday's subject was aroused by the dual effects of purple and yellow, which are exact opposites on the color spectrum and therefore stimulating to the eye in combination.

Purple clothing speaks passionately and stirs the senses. In the fantasy described above, the subtle sensuality of the purples played off the vibrancy of the yellows. Purple's deep, spiritual power merged with yellow's blatant warmth.

Mauve and violet are the colors of dreams and spirituality, which is why those in the arts or philosophy are fond of purple. Deep purple reveals an individual who has eccentric traits but is warm-blooded. Harkening back to early Rome, when pounds and pounds of mollusks had to be crushed to produce a small amount of this costly coloring, purple has also been known as the color of royalty. Its royal implications also make purple the color of a person with high self-esteem. Throughout Jewish history, the most honored rabbis were always cloaked in purple robes, as were Roman rulers. Clothed in a purple velvet robe, we, too, can feel an air of regality and opulence.

Purple also carries with it an air of aloofness. This association heightens its effect and elevates the woman in purple clothing to a position of unattainable worthiness.

Wearing purple or violet can inspire passion within us as well as in those encountering us. Purple also tends to be very theatrical, since it combines the fire of red and the tranquillity of blue.

Lavender and violet are particularly ethereal, usually the colors of dreamers. Deep shades of purple appeal to refined minds and souls. Violet is romantic, passionate, and magical. Plum and heather suggest high economic status because of the exclusivity of the color.

In general, those drawn to the color purple are very likely creative and passionate, with a heightened sense of spirituality.

SERENE GREEN

Green is the most relaxing color to the eye because the rays of light from green focus directly on the retina. Light green tones lull the heart rate and offer pleasant, almost euphoric feelings of serenity, which is why they put people in the "green room" before they are about to be interviewed on television.

Soft greens send signals of compassion and communicate that the wearer is nurturing and open-minded. Green is a healing color, suggestive of someone in touch with the environment. Emotionally, green rejuvenates and offers the promise of a fresh start.

The color of trees and plant life, green represents growth and fertility. Considered a lucky color to the Irish, green was banned by the early Christians because it was used in pagan ceremonies.

On the negative side, green is also associated with jealousy, alien beings, and nausea. And there are certain shades of green that are quite unflattering to some complexions.

Still, green is the harbinger of renewal. A woman garbed in green appears young and open-minded. However, these same qualities prevent green from being a "power" color. Its freshness implies a lack of maturity and expertise. The Wagner Institute found that green is the worst color for soliciting donations—unless you're a Girl Scout. It is also probably a poor choice for a job interview or to promote a product.

Dark green, hunter green, and blue greens are colors of prestige and high society, but only when worn for recreational sports or in nonconservative businesses.

Green is often popular in times of economic prosperity because of its link to the color of money.

VIBRANT ORANGE

Orange is an audacious, energizing color, and the people who wear it tend not to care what others think. That may be a particular advantage, because women who wear orange are often not taken seriously anyway—at least not in business. Since orange is associated with

Halloween, pumpkins, and clowns, it detracts from an otherwise businesslike demeanor.

On the other hand, the woman who likes orange is probably a warm, mercurial individual.

The various hues of orange each send distinctive messages. An orange-tinted peach or coral signifies someone who is down-to-earth; others tend to warm up to her quickly. Bright, clear orange or shocking orange attracts attention, but in a friendly way. Unlike red, it lends the wearer a more approachable demeanor. An orange shirt or suit exclaims that we are outgoing and spontaneous. Warmer oranges and muted shades such as pumpkin and coral are more sophisticated than shocking or bright oranges. Earth-tone oranges tend to portray us as down-to-earth and environmentally conscious.

NATURAL BROWN

Brown is an informal color that does not command much power. It certainly does not have the presence of navy or black. Brown is synonymous with the earth and soil and thus is the most basic of nature's colors. Because brown was worn by peasants in the Middle Ages, we also associate it with humility. During the Depression, people wore brown to disguise clothes that were infrequently washed or stained. But brown is a pleasing color—a mixture of orange and black, it makes us feel secure and sedate without being stuffy. There is a particular warmth and sensuality to brown when it's softened with red or orange.

When we wear deep brown, we're perceived as reliable. In a brown suit, a woman comes across as stable and supportive. Brown is a nonthreatening color, and people tend to feel safe around others who favor it. Warm shades of bronze (suntan, terra-cotta, or brick brown) tend to put others at ease. We probably open up more around a woman who wears these tones, thus making them good candidates to stimulate conversation.

Since there are so many different shades of brown, individual responses to each vary. Rose brown, bisque cream, champagne, toast, and tan signal a highly educated and financially successful individual. A woman should wear these colors if she wants to increase her perceived social status. Yet because they're neutral, such colors do not convey much emotion. To infuse brown with more feeling or vitality, consult the Complementary Color Chart on page 23.

GRAY AREAS

Because the color gray is associated with the brain (gray matter) and "gray areas" that exercise the intellect more than "black and white" issues—and because it's also linked with age/wisdom (gray hair, a "graybeard")—gray is favored by artists, intellectuals, and philosophers. Studies show that artists are more creative when working in a gray environment or during foggy, overcast weather than in brighter, more stimulating settings.

Gray is also a color of refinement, class, and efficiency. Wearing a medium to deep gray suit in a luxurious fabric will communicate economic and social mobility and give off strong messages of power.

Silver is a brighter form of gray, and shades of silver or platinum are a sign of affluence. One thinks of "silver screens" and "clouds with silver linings." Steel gray and green gray have negative associations since they occur in nature's palette during treacherous weather conditions.

Tints of gray have distinctly different meanings. A dark gray, as in gray flannel, is a serious, mature shade. One expects a woman wearing this color to be very responsible. Gray can also be a sign of depression. A light brownish gray can make one appear old, weary, and downtrodden; it not only represents ashes and death but is an unflattering shade on most people.

Gray is black and white mixed together. In some ways it is an uncertain color, again probably thanks to "gray area" allusions. Gray is also a color of fear.

Because gray is midway between white and black, it straddles the fence and asks for no commitments. When worn head to toe, gray can wash out the complexion and make the wearer look ashen. So gray should be accented with an enlivening color—such as pink, white, or red—near the face.

GUIDE TO COLORS FOR EVERY OCCASION

Colors to Wear on a First Date (colors that make an impression)

- ◆ *Yellow-based reds (true or lacquer red, primary red).* Preferably in soft fabrics like cashmere, silk, or light wool and mixed with black (to speed up adrenaline and heart-beat and demand full attention). Men are inherently attracted to yellow reds, which have an intense and arousing effect.

- ◆ *Yellow-based pinks and peach.* Elicits attention. Enhances perceptions of romance, lull the heart.

- ◆ *Midrange red violet and pastel red violet.* Good response from upper-socioeconomic men, radiates spirituality, illuminates the personality.

◆ *Muted midrange rose and pastel rose.* Good response, elicits affection.

◆ *Black.* Mysterious, erotic, emanates a sense of the unknown and the forbidden.

◆ *Pale blue or deep sky blue.* Generates affection and romantic fantasies; calms and tranquilizes.

Colors to Wear on Romantic Dates

◆ *Scarlet, matador red, yellow-based red.* Arousing and exciting.

◆ *Rose.* Suggests an ethereal beauty.

◆ *Crimson.* Inspires eroticism, passion, and sexual energy.

◆ *Deep blue red.* Conveys confidence, sophistication, and warmth; distorts perception of time.

◆ *Pale and deep red violets.* Inspires nostalgia and romance.

◆ *Aqua.* Tender yet stimulating.

◆ *Sky blue.* Has a lulling effect.

◆ *Muted, pastel blue.* Elicits kindness and playfulness.

◆ *Pale, yellow-based pink.* Flirtatious, playful.

◆ *Pale green.* Sense of sweetness; projects a nature-loving individual.

◆ *Pink, cornflower blue, coral, apricot.* Feminine; draws men closer, projects warmth and emotional availability.

Colors to Wear on a Blind Date (when one is hopeful yet cautious)

◆ *Sky blue.* Connotes freedom, independence, a sense of well-being.

◆ *Muted pastel blue.* Femininity and trust.

◆ *Cornflower blue.* Suggests kindness and honesty.

◆ *Yellow-based pink.* Incites passion without being overtly sexual.

◆ *Blue, red, wine.* Signifies courage and confidence.

◆ *Terra-cotta, brick, suntan, peach, and apricot.* Sends out signals of compassion, earthiness.

Colors for Brainstorming or Creative Endeavors

◆ *Orchid.* Color of illumination.

◆ *Blue-based pinks—pale to deep pink.* Inspires creativity.

◆ *Lavender.* Adds spirituality.

◆ *Pale and sky blue, cornflower and bright deep blue.* Encourages fantasy.

◆ *Tan.* Elicits information and keeps conversation flowing.

◆ *Purple.* Stirs the senses and generates passion.

◆ *Light to warm gray.* Enhances artistic development.

◆ *Red violet.* Suggests tranquillity and passion at the same time.

◆ *Flashes or accents of red and yellow.* For stimulation.

Colors for Interacting with Women
(colors women respond well to)

◆ *Terra-cotta.* Women warm up to this color quickly; has a sensuous, earthy appeal.

◆ *Clear or shocking orange.* Vibrant and energetic; inspires a bond.

◆ *Red violet.* Great fashion color; signifies intelligence.

◆ *Violet or deep purple.* Theatrical and dramatic; shows warm-bloodedness.

◆ *White.* Neutral, calming, indicates you are trustworthy.

◆ *Blue green, jade, or light green.* Lulls the heart rate, produces feeling of serenity, sends signals of compassion and nurturing.

◆ *Blue-based pastel pink.* Sends out nonthreatening signals of compassion and innocence; great female bonding color; offers a sense of trust and concern for emotions.

◆ *Blue-based strong pink.* Affectionate yet fashion conscious.

◆ *Pale pink or warm pink.* Puts women at ease.

◆ *Deep blue red.* Signifies courage.

◆ *Turquoise or pastel aqua.* Elicits positive response; puts women at ease to open up more.

◆ *Muted and pastel rose.* Colors of affection.

Colors of the Fashion Conscious

◆ *Lipstick red.* Implies strength and authority.

◆ *Fuchsia.* Vivacious and dynamic.

◆ *Deep purple.* Indicative of creativity and artistic power.

DRESS CODE

♦ *Pale and pastel purple.* Spiritual.

♦ *Muted and clear orange.* Warmth and earthiness.

♦ *Raspberry.* To appear friendly and intelligent.

Colors for Interacting Socially and Professionally with Men (colors men respond well to)

♦ *Yellow.* Holds their attention and keeps them alert; indicates the start of something new.

♦ *Yellow-based reds.* Keeps conversation going.

♦ *Matador red.* Bespeaks confidence.

♦ *Burgundy.* Reflects class and sophistication and will draw out these types of individuals.

♦ *Midrange blues.* Puts others at ease; allows interactions to go smoothly.

♦ *Sky blue.* Calms.

♦ *Navy blue.* Signals you want to be taken seriously; inspires others to listen to what you have to say; shows that you're trustworthy.

♦ *Blue-based reds.* Connotes intelligence and femininity.

◆ *Red plum.* Suggests strength and creativity.

◆ *Tan worn with bisque, cream, or camel.* Very tactile; sophisticated, yet shows you're approachable.

Colors for Job Interviews (conservative professions)

◆ *Charcoal gray.* Communicates power and success and shows that you are serious.

◆ *Navy blue.* Authoritative; signals that you're trustworthy, responsible, organized, and well balanced.

◆ *Royal blue.* Affirmative; suggests faithfulness and trust-worthiness.

◆ *Black with neutral tones.* Conveys a sense of power and intensity.

Colors for Job Interviews (creative professions)

◆ *Yellow touches.* Shows alertness and a cheerful personality.

◆ *Pink.* Calms and makes others respond with kindness.

◆ *Black and white.* Contrast signifies sharpness of the mind.

- *Cornflower blue.* Conveys a sense of whimsy and imagination.

Colors for Business Meetings or Lunches (with colleagues or clients)

- *Black.* Power.

- *Navy blue.* Trustworthiness.

- *Royal blue.* Sends out signals of goodwill.

- *Deep gray.* Bespeaks success and strength.

- *Camel or shades of brown.* Appears nonthreatening, stable, supportive, and reliable.

- *Terra-cotta or brick.* Projects warmth and sensuality.

- *Blue reds.* Indicates warmth, vitality.

Colors for Traveling or Shopping

- *Terra-cotta.* Indicates friendliness.

- *Orange- and blue-based reds.* Gets the attention you might want or need.

◆ *Peach.* Elicits concern.

◆ *Pinks.* Projects youth and innocence.

◆ *Yellows.* Elicit help, to get attention quickly.

Colors to Wear When Promoting or Selling a Product

◆ *True blue or lighter shades of blue.* To inspire trust.

◆ *Orange.* Friendly, appeals to all.

◆ *Yellow.* Cheerful and stimulating.

◆ *Blue-based pinks.* To calm and inspire others.

Colors to Wear at Dinner Parties

◆ *Touches of red and bright yellow.* To stimulate.

◆ *Soft blue.* To calm guests.

◆ *Soft yellow and pink.* Puts guests in a cheerful mood.

◆ *Orange.* Sends out warmth and friendliness to cheer guests.

◆ *White.* Says you are open to conversation.

Colors to Wear for Public Speaking

◆ *Red-black blues.* Generates excitement.

◆ *Scarlet accents.* Draws attention; elicits compassion.

◆ *Black.* Powerful, dynamic.

◆ *Blue- or tomato-based red.* Generates excitement, holds attention.

◆ *Yellow.* Holds attention.

◆ *Deep or vivid pinks.* Indicates passion for your topic.

◆ *Navy to midrange blues.* Inspires trustworthiness.

◆ *Royal or lapis blue.* Shows goodwill, trustworthiness, introspection.

◆ *Blue green.* Very popular color; people respond favorably to those who wear to it.

Colors with an Upper-Class Appeal (to be worn when applying for a loan, attending a board meeting, or discussing a financial endeavor)

- Burgundy

- Maroon

- Dark blue green

- Red plum

- Blue-based red

- Dark green

- Dark blue

- Royal blue

- Bisque

- Cream, tan

- Champagne

Chapter 3

Fashion Seductions: Sex Appeal and Style

"No fashion is ever a success unless it is used as a form of seduction."

—*Christian Dior*

It is spring. The doors of a trendy restaurant on the west side of Los Angeles swing open to admit a woman so jarringly seductive that every head in the place turns to watch her as she is shown to a table. A décolletage bustier beaded in a swirl of jewel colors clings to the contours of her curves. A chiffon scarf drapes fluidly over her shoulders, and a pair of slim black chiffon trousers suggest the shape of lithe legs beneath. Silk boots hug her ankles. Her ebony hair is swept up seductively in a chignon. She feels the eyes of everyone in the restaurant and basks in their admiration.

In a suburban living room hundreds of miles from the chic eateries of West Los Angeles, a woman returning from work lays down her briefcase and glances through the mail. As she takes off her conservative suit jacket, she picks up a Victoria's Secret catalog and sits on the couch to flip through it. Lacy French-cut underwear in shades of scarlet and black catches her eye. She wonders if anyone would be the wiser were she to wear such enticing garments underneath her high-collared silk blouses and tailored suits.

Regardless of how liberated we are, most of us indulge in

55

provocative dressing from time to time. Sometimes it's a straightforward attempt to arouse a current lover—or attract a potential one. Often it's a more private expression of sensuality that is not necessarily shared at all. There are also those who use sexually explicit clothing to express a hunger for power and equality. They flaunt their feminine attributes not to seduce or manipulate but to proclaim their female potency.

Whatever her motives, a woman will always have an abundance of seductive styles from which to choose. Each season the fashion industry creates alluring new fashions intended for "the eye of the beholder," whether it's a strapless dress that exposes gleaming bare shoulders, a plunging neckline that shows off the shadows of cleavage, or a backless blouse that draws the eye to the sinuous curve of the back and spine.

The truth of the matter is that revealing fashions make a woman feel sexually attractive. Navel-skimming sweaters, thigh-high hemlines, and thong swimsuits are essential props in the quest for sexual attention. But are you aware of what other messages these overt clothes send?

When we wear provocative clothing, our body language is subtly altered. A woman does not stroll down the street the same way in a microminiskirt and high heels as she does in a pair of jeans and boots. Walking and moving in such styles changes a woman's posture, endowing each movement with a seductive, contrived air. When we wear body-conscious clothing, we divert attention from our faces to our bodies. Clinging clothing molds, lifts, and thrusts out our body parts, unlike softer, draped clothing, which draws attention to our face. While this may indeed be the intended effect, there's a fine but critical line between vulgarity and sensuality; it's important to be aware of the subtleties communicated by various outfits.

The effects of provocative clothing can be tempered or height-

ened, depending on what the clothing is paired with. For example, slim miniskirts worn with a loose-fitting or tailored blouse, jacket, or T-shirt are alluring, while the same miniskirt paired with a tight Lycra bodysuit or top looks flimsy and suggestive. Short skirts are fine with a pair of opaque tights and flats, but put on seamed, lace, or fishnet stockings and high heels and the message is something quite different. Catsuits are slinky, sleek, and blatantly seductive on their own, but when worn with a sarong or a long blazer, they look chic and proper.

Cashmere sweaters denote softness and gently emphasize the breasts. They're erotic, but softly so. A wrap sweater in Lycra or another clinging fabric makes a more overt sexual statement, caressing the body as it divides and lifts the breasts.

Among the most titillating garments are those that invite the viewer to linger on a particular part of the body. Often they both cover and reveal at the same time. A perfect example is the G-string, which provides an amusing game of hide-and-seek for both the wearer and the voyeur. The G-string not only divides the derriere but also causes the viewer to contemplate where it ultimately leads.

In fact, what is most sexy is the mysterious and the hidden. For example, a wrap that slips off to show the nape of the neck makes that unclothed part of the body more seductive. Revealing a little is, and always has been, much more tantalizing than baring everything. A long dress that caresses our curves and has a plunging back or a slit up the side is much more interesting to the eye than a short, clinging Lycra dress. A silk dress with lace insets in the right place hints at our sexuality and is far more seductive and refined than a transparent lace dress. The woman whose clothes cover—even if just barely—her erotic zones is viewed as more intelligent and sensuous than the one whose clothing sends an unsubtle message of availability by clearly revealing those areas.

The message expressed in seductive fashion ought to be whispered, not shouted. Any outfit that displays the body too obviously loses its allure—because when the mystery is lost, so is the interest.

REVEALING PARTS OF THE BODY

Subtly drawing attention to the most attractive features of your body is the secret to achieving an alluring look. You may be blessed with a swanlike neck or a lovely swell of décolletage; or perhaps you have a narrow waist and curvaceous hips. Choosing clothes that emphasize your unique attributes will create a more attractive image than simply buying the latest sexy fashion. Whether you want to show off a sinuous back, a tight, curvy backside, well-shaped cleavage, enviably long legs, or a narrow waist, you should be aware that each erogenous zone has its own set of hidden psychological implications.

THE BEHIND

In the sixteenth century, women wore padded garments to give the illusion of a more rounded bottom. Today, bustles, poufs, and trains that direct the eyes toward and accentuate a woman's buttocks accomplish the same end. The appearance of ample hips hint at fecundity, whereas a woman with slim hips (perhaps one who has dieted and diminished her curves) seems to be denying her reproductive desires.

THE LEGS

Men have always found the flash of a curvaceous limb titillating. Historically, short skirts, and even those exposing only glimpses of the leg, were reserved for women on public view—prostitutes and showgirls. The mainstream popularity of shorter skirts can be attributed directly to the advent of leggings or tights in the early 1800s. Because the skin of the leg was covered with opaque leggings, shorter skirts became socially acceptable—at least for young girls. Since they didn't pose a sexual threat, schoolgirls were permitted to wear skirts of a previously scandalous length, probably no more than six inches above the ankle.

However, legs were still kept under wraps until the turn of this century, an outward sign of the continued repression of woman's sexuality. But when sheer stockings finally came on the scene in the early 1900s, their back seams invited the viewer to dwell on a woman's ankle and calf. The stocking and garter draw the eye to the top of the thigh, the symbolic gateway to sexual pleasure as well as one of the most sensitive areas of the body. It wasn't until the 1920s, however, that women had the freedom to wear fashions that allowed for more ease of movement—and showed off their legs. Today, long diaphanous skirts that silhouette the legs allow a previously forbidden glimpse of this sensual part of the body.

The deeply slit evening dress is another provocative look. Men's eyes are drawn immediately to the side of the dress, as they follow the slit to the top of the wearer's thigh; they may never even notice the rest of the gown.

BREASTS

Breasts are probably the single most potent symbol of female power and sexuality, and they're literally popping up and out on fashion runways and the pages of slick magazines. Breast cones—conical-shaped decorative brassiere attachments—are the most brazen sexual accoutrements to come along since Cleopatra's serpentine breastplates. Because the breast cone is a metaphor for the male phallic symbol, the more pointed and longer they are, the more arresting they are.

Likewise, the more pronounced the appearance of the breast, the greater the impact. Rounded swells emerging from strapless bustiers and décolletage dresses send a double message of sexual availability and the potency of our gender.

Flashing one's breasts by unbuttoning the top buttons of a blouse is a gesture of sexual assertion and may also be a way of conveying that one is proud to be a woman. Breasts radiate warmth and womanhood and, of course, provide sustenance to newborns. This powerful, life-giving function is a hidden source of envy for men and is inextricably entwined in the mystique surrounding women's breasts.

Styles that emphasize the breasts include strapless gowns and bustiers, which give the illusion that there is nothing holding up the dress except the swell of the breast beneath. Long, slinky, strapless

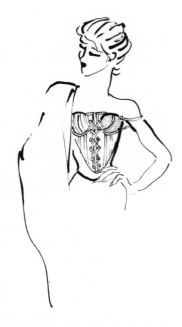

dresses that slide loosely around a woman's breasts look as though they might be easily peeled off or slide down on their own to reveal this highly erogenous zone. Similarly, off-the-shoulder dresses subtly suggest that as soon as we bend down or lean over, the view will become even more compelling.

Even an off-the-shoulder peasant blouse with flounces or ruffles is not without sexual charm. Peasant clothing has an alluring innocence that makes its sexual appeal even more tantalizing. The country look of a laced-up corset in floral tones, ruffles, and flounce suggests virginity; short, baby-doll skirts also bespeak a sexual innocence; and sheer organza blouses are sweet yet revealing, an enticing combination.

On the other hand, the eroticism of the breast is obliterated when it is displayed so nonchalantly as to inspire shock rather than lust or titillation—as in certain outrageous, fully topless designer creations.

THE ARMS

Even the arm can be an interesting, if subtle, erotic appendage. A well-developed arm that tapers to a fragile wrist becomes downright sexy when encased in a pair of long, sensual gloves. Gloves are both ladylike and yet suggestive, as they are associated with the striptease.

THE PHYSICALLY FIT BODY

Arousing the desire of the opposite sex is not the only function of seductive fashions. Many of us feel that form-fitting clothing gives us a powerful edge. "If you've got it, flaunt it" was a recurring refrain of the last decade. Body-revealing clothing allowed women to show their strength as well as their femininity.

Tight dresses and streamlined suits call attention to the bodies that many of us spend hours tightening, toning, and shaping. The 1980s and 1990s introduced dresses that encased women like mummies, some complete with sewn-in girdles. Sinewy, aerobicized bodies were shown to advantage in garments held together and molded by clinging strips of stretch fabrics. Muscles and curves sprang out of unexpected cutouts and slashes. Designers Azzedine Alaia's and Hervé Leger's fashions, for example, mold bodies with fabrics that seem to melt into the wearer's curves.

The body-hugging catsuit, or unitard, is one of the most emotionally charged body-conscious garments. It is symbolic of the unpredictable cat, which purrs one moment and bares its claws the next. In *Batman*, Catwoman is sexy but treacherous, a criminal forever trying to lure Batman into her lair (and nearly succeeding). The catsuit captures this aura of the independent, seductive animal who attacks when threatened; the woman who wears a catsuit is seen as sensual yet potentially dangerous.

The catsuit is a second skin, and it derives its shape entirely from the lines of the body it encases. Launched into fashion originally by designers Courrèges and Rudi Gernreich, the catsuit was the epitome of fashionably androgynous attire in 1969. Gernreich promoted this audacious garment as an emblem of liberation for both men and women. Courrèges felt it freed women from the issue of skirt lengths; all they needed to do was wear a bodysuit underneath their skirt. The catsuit retreated for a time, only to resurge after the glitter of the 1980s; it was reintroduced by Christian Lacroix in 1990, who—along with the many designers of exercise wear—made it popular again.

Although styles that define every bodily contour can send a message of self-confidence, power, and dynamism, they may also make the wearer feel highly vulnerable, since no part of the body's shape is concealed. Ultimately the fashion statement transmitted in "styles for the physically fit" depends on a woman's attitude toward her body and how she feels about going public with it.

UNDERWEAR AS OUTERWEAR

Designer Jean Paul Gaultier launched the phenomenon of lingerie as outerwear when he designed the outrageous costumes Madonna wore on her 1988 concert tour. The specter of the singer strutting around the stage with her conical bra tops assaulted the eyes and shocked the sensibilities, as she no doubt intended. Yet it wasn't long before a modified version of these overtly sexual fashions was being worn by women everywhere.

Madonna notwithstanding, the lingerie look is not a recent innovation. Marilyn Monroe, for example, favored short, lingerielike styles that signaled her sexual vulnerability. Short, strapless dresses with underwire push-up bras allow us to slip into that docile yet sultry persona. They signify an innocent sexuality that exudes femininity and charm. The smoothness of satin corset dresses also suggests vulnerability because of satin's association with the smoothness of skin. Wearing such styles is the most unabashedly sensual way to flaunt one's breasts, short of baring them.

Yves Saint Laurent introduced the slip dress with boned corsets in 1977. Boned white cotton corsets with eyelets conjure up the conflicting images of innocence and naughtiness, harkening back to their origins as proper Victorian-era lingerie. In the eighteenth century, silky, seductive lingerie was considered improper, as it was associated exclusively with promiscuous women.

Lingerie, however, has always been a tool of overt flirtation. Anne Bancroft's seduction of Dustin Hoffman in *The Graduate* in her leopard print lingerie was forever imprinted in the minds of 1960s moviegoers, as was the image of Elizabeth Taylor's satin-slipped Maggie "the cat" in the film version of *Cat on a Hot Tin Roof.*

Wearing lingerie as outerwear sends the most mixed of messages. It says a woman feels secure enough about her body and sexuality to flaunt it and divulge its secrets. Yet she also projects a vulnerability, since she is quite literally exposed. This erotic vulnerability stems from the personal and intimate nature of lingerie—items usually seen only in private moments. Wearing lingerie as a fashion statement shatters cultural and fashion taboos by allowing others a glimpse of our most intimate self.

The erotic appeal of lingerie is also connected to the feel of sensuous fabrics against the skin. The physical stimulus of silk, satin, or velvet arouses the wearer's senses, making her feel caressed and rendering her more sensual and attuned to tactile stimuli.

When worn outside the bedroom for evening or as daywear, lingerie sends boudoir signals of intimacy. Details such as lace ribbons and bows at the border of lingerie or clothing lead others to fantasize about what is being concealed underneath.

SEDUCTIVE FABRICS

It's not difficult to interpret the erotic meanings of lingerie and the fabrics associated with it. Lace, often used to edge the bottom of teddies, dresses, and bodysuits, has been used to titillate for centuries. In the 1900s, lace-edged pantaloons peeked out from under skirts and incited men to such a degree that the garments were eventually prohibited! A glimpse of lace under a subdued business jacket or evening coat is likewise erotic because it offers a subtle invitation into forbidden territory. The silk of slips, camisoles, and panties (especially the aptly named peau de soie, or "skin of silk") represents the suppleness of a woman's supple skin. And fur is one of the most erotic materials of all, reminiscent of a woman's pubic hair. The animal magnetism and lust associated with fur can be seen to represent a woman's baser drives.

EROTIC DETAILS

Often it's the tiniest details of an outfit that have the greatest erotic impact. An astute fashion consumer will pay as much attention to detail in selecting a particular garment as her intrigued admirer will once she's wearing it. Even the seemingly insignificant fastenings on a woman's clothing can telegraph unintended messages about her sexual attitudes and proclivities.

In a "civilized" society, public sexuality is unthinkable; propriety dictates that the body be at least partially covered at all times. Thus the visible fastenings on articles of clothing are associated with basic sexual inhibitions waiting to be set free with the simple act of unfastening.

In general, garments with snaps, ties, and bows allude to the fact that one's sexuality and passions are tied up—waiting to be loosened. These fasteners, as well as zippers, have a sexual power all their own, as they invite the observer to participate in a game of seduction. If you wear an outfit from a designer known for his or her bold, bondage-inspired details, you signal a sexual disposition that is likewise bold and direct. These garments convey that you're not one to waste time or play games, since the fastenings on them are easily undone.

But if you choose clothing with more discreet attachments— sweaters with tiny pearl buttons or elastic fastenings—which require time and patience to undo, you are likely to be considered a more sophisticated, discreet lover. The same could be said if you prefer clothing with concealed buttons and zippers.

Styles that zip up the front are subtly seductive. The scubalike suit or jacket that ushered in the early nineties was a good example; not only does this garment firmly mold the body parts, but the zipper suggests that with one swift tug, your entire body will be revealed. This image is further reinforced when the wearer, consciously or unconsciously, fiddles with the zipper. In fact, J. C. Flugel, author of *The Psychology of Clothing,* has suggested that idly playing with the buttons or zippers on one's clothing is a form of masturbation, and that the button passing through the buttonhole is symbolic of coitus.

Dresses, pants, and other garments that lace or snap up the front or the back are advertising that they can be undone promptly. At the same time, however, they may suggest that you need assistance in the untying ceremony.

Loosely tied garments constitute an invitation to this ceremony. Bows, in particular, conjure the fantasy of "unwrapping" a gift. Leather corsets with hooks, merry widows, dresses fastened with buckles, and hardware corset dresses that lace up the front not only alter the shape of the women who wear them, they also provide undressing and dominatrix fantasies for the viewer.

The sight of jewels and pearls on bare skin is also enticing—especially jewel-encrusted straps that stretch against bare skin or glimmering pearls that drape across the back. Jewelry on dresses, especially silk or satin lingerie—such as slip dresses—implies that the woman inside the dress is an expensive package. Since jewelry has always been both a desirable gift and a luxury item, a woman ensconced in a jeweled dress, bustier, or bodysuit sends out the subliminal message that she is a precious commodity.

Ankle bracelets enjoyed a vogue during World War II, when fashionable clothing and elegant fabrics were scarce. Unable to indulge themselves in glamorous clothes, young women wore thin gold ankle bracelets on their legs to captivate admirers.

A second wave of popularity for ankle bracelets came in the 1950s, when these thin-linked bracelets adorned with pearls and hearts were popular among teenage girls as a romantic token. Wearing the ankle bracelet on the left ankle conveyed that a girl belonged to one boy alone; if worn on the right ankle, the bracelet signaled that although she belonged to someone, he could be easily supplanted under the right circumstances.

MIXED MESSAGES

The line between a subtly inviting look and an overly provocative one is fine indeed. Too often the woman who opts for an extremely seductive image runs the risk of being misperceived. When she dons a revealing dress or slinky sweater, she may unknowingly be sending the message that her body is her only valuable asset or that all she is interested in is a sexual encounter. The image of the seductress is a double-edged sword. On the one hand it attracts attention.

On the other it implies that a woman considers her body a commodity, an attribute more significant than any other, including intelligence. A brazen image will turn heads, but is it really the kind of recognition that is desired?

There is often a strong disparity between how we perceive ourselves and how others see us. For example, when a woman chooses a dress with a plunging neckline or stiletto heels for a date, she may simply be trying to look attractive. But her date may interpret her clothing choices as an invitation—one that is not, in fact, being extended. Many men perceive sexy clothes as concrete evidence of promiscuity.

"When a woman tries to be alluring to men, it is inevitable that she is going to annoy other women."—Isaac Mizrahi

---

While provocative clothing holds a fascination for members of the opposite sex, it can also create barriers between members of our own sex. Women tend to view other women who wear revealing clothing as inconsiderate, insincere, and generally less likable than those who dress conservatively. Consider the following scenario:

Two women walk into a dinner party. The first wears a beige cashmere sweater dress with a shawl wrapped around her shoulders, the other a black velvet microminidress with a deeply scalloped back that reveals the cleavage of her derriere. The tight bodice of her dress emphasizes her ample breasts. Anyone whose eyes fell upon the second woman focused on either her chest or the nakedness of her back.

Those looking at the first woman tend to see her face first and her outfit as part of her overall appearance. As the evening progresses, the seductively dressed woman begins to feel quite uncomfortable, as much because of the cold response she receives from the other women in the room as from the overly solicitous attention of the men. The outrageousness of her outfit obscures her otherwise warm and lively personality. In self-defense, she begins to put up her own emotional barrier and become arrogant, standoffish, and critical of others at the party. By contrast, the woman in the beige cashmere sweater dress is approached more warmly by male and female guests alike, which makes her feel more relaxed and open.

As they leave the gathering, one guest asks his wife if she has been offended by the male attention showered upon the woman in the black micromini. The wife responds that she felt embarrassed to see a woman so hungry for attention.

Her reaction is not uncommon. Many women feel that an overtly sexual image demeans not only the wearer but all women, because such a look plays into the long-held stereotypes of woman as either whore or Madonna. On the other hand, there are those who claim that such a "prudish" reaction occurs only in those afraid of their own exhibitionist tendencies, which lie in the "shadow" part of every woman.

When we dress seductively, are we alienating women in order to please men? Is a man's response to our appearance so different from a woman's? The results of a University of Missouri study might surprise you. Twenty men and women were asked to rate the attractiveness of the same woman dressed in both provocative and nonprovocative outfits. Each person in the sample was shown a series of photographs. In one photograph the woman wore a T-shirt over a bra, in another no bra and a wet T-shirt, in yet another a buttoned shirt, and in the last a shirt that was unbuttoned to the midriff. Surprisingly, when viewing photographs of the deliberately provocative outfits, men *did not perceive an increase* in the woman's attractiveness, and women perceived a *decrease* in attractiveness.

Again, when it comes to sexually explicit styles, it seems both men and women respond most favorably to those looks that represent some degree of moderation—old-fashioned as that may sound.

EXHIBITIONISM

Exhibitionism is not the same as seduction. Exhibitionists use their provocative clothing to startle and cause outrage, not necessarily to gain sexual partners. Their clothes have a theatrical flair, often crossing the line into the realm of the ridiculous. Shocking others with their wild style affords such women a power that may elude them in other areas of their lives.

Typical exhibitionist wear includes Lycra dresses with plunging necklines or backs; double-breasted blazers worn with lace, cleavage-exposing camisoles or no shirt at all; dramatic, sweeping capes; bizarre hats; and any style of short, ultratight miniskirt. Dressing this way makes women in the public eye the perfect target for the Worst Dressed List—but, of course, that's really the point.

The exhibitionist's outfits telegraph a need to be recognized for her body, and her sexy demeanor suggests this is the attribute she values most. She desperately needs to shock and get attention, because this makes her feel important.

Women who exploit their bodies in this way are often driven by an inner rage. Consciously or not, the exhibitionist announces to onlookers that other parts of her life are unfulfilling and that the attention she attracts by dressing outrageously fills the void.

Such neediness is especially common among performers. At a recent film premiere, an actress well known for craving attention and publicity felt she was being overshadowed by other celebrities in the crowd. She became petulant and annoyed as she jockeyed to be noticed. In a last-ditch effort to gain an audience, she threw off her dress, revealing a jewel-encrusted bra top and a G-string that provocatively exposed her buttocks. When she leapt onto a table and began to dance, she created the hoped-for commotion, as the paparazzi rushed to snap pictures. Finally satisfied, she got down from the table and walked away.

Although others expect the behavior of these "fashion shockers" to be as outlandish as their clothing, in fact exhibitionist fashions often mask the wearer's true inclinations. While a flashy, lusty image leads onlookers to draw certain obvious conclusions, many exhibitionist women either have little interest in sex or find it difficult or even impossible to be responsive.

"Women like to please. They like to dress for somebody else. It could be a friend, it could be a husband, it could be a lover, it can be somebody to conquer."—Valentino

---

Certainly women have reached the point where our sexual attractiveness is not the only attribute we value in ourselves. But this doesn't mean there aren't times when a woman wants to feel and appear sexy—for the lover in her life, for an anonymous onlooker, or just for herself. Our sexuality is a vital part of who we are, and expressing it can be healthy, playful, and invigorating. Still, revealing our sexual selves through the styles we choose is a question of nuance. Just as we take care not to come on too strong in our relationships with friends and lovers, we must take similar precautions when it comes to selecting sensual apparel. Otherwise our quest for sexual attention can backfire, leaving us to wonder where we went wrong. For all our hard-won liberation, it may be that our mothers and grandmothers had it right when they counseled us on appropriate attire for attracting a man: Leave them guessing.

Chapter 4

The Masculine Mystique: Women in Men's Clothes

"Men are men, but Man is a woman."
—*G. K. Chesterton*

Wearing man-tailored clothing can endow a woman with a sense of confident potency. Drawn to suits and trousers not only for their comfort but for their ubiquitous phallic symbolism, the woman who wears pants and shoulder pads both feels and appears stronger. And it's no mystery why we would want to be invested with male qualities, since historically men have been afforded a range of opportunities and privileges denied to women. Donning men's clothing is a symbolic way to inherit this privileged position.

Wearing the pants—or, more precisely, the cuffed trousers—in the family or corporation is now a woman's prerogative. As women grow more independent and more in touch with their masculine sides, this new his-for-her style has become increasingly popular. But like all the fashion choices we make, this one can be a double-edged sword. To certain onlookers we may appear competent and commanding in our male-influenced styles; to others we may seem intimidating and lacking in traditionally feminine attributes.

Like most fashion news, however, cross-dressing goes back centuries. French novelist George Sand (the pseudonym of Amandine Aurore Lucie Dupin) wore male attire as early as the 1830s to protest the unequal status of women. In the 1910s and 1920s, daring European and American women, most of whom were associated with the feminist movement or avant-garde philosophical and art movements, delighted in shocking mainstream society by wearing men's suits, ties, hats, and shoes. Their intent was obvious: to shake up the status quo and declare their independence from rigid gender roles.

Not until several decades later, in the 1940s, did society at large begin to accept women in trousers. Even then, however, there were restrictions on when trousers were appropriate and what kind was acceptable. Women did not appear at work or in the street in pants, although they could wear them to garden, lounge around the house, horseback ride, or go to the beach. Wearing pants for such activities acknowledged the functional quality of men's clothing, as compared with the purely ornamental purpose of women's.

Celebrities like Marlene Dietrich, Katharine Hepburn, Rosalind Russell, and Laurel Bacall helped broaden the acceptability of male look-alike styles. In their chic, mannish pants suits they emanated a cool assurance yet remained seductive and feminine. In fact, the juxtaposition of contrasting elements—masculine clothing with feminine hairstyles, makeup, and contours—created a unique eroticism.

The designer responsible for easing women into pants for good was André Courrèges, who in the 1960s held that a contemporary woman needed the comfort and functionality of pants to survive in

an electronic age. Courrèges's tube-shaped pants in white became the foundation of his collections. At about the same time, Cerruti introduced matching suits for men and women, and Yves Saint Laurent invented the woman's tuxedo.

Over the years, Giorgio Armani, the acknowledged czar of menswear-inspired clothes for women, has added masculine accessories to the now commonplace trousers. These include spectators, loafers, and wing-tip shoes; baseball caps; military-style berets; argyle socks; vests; leather driving gloves; ties; and sweaters tied around the waist.

Today, women have adopted a wide range of male accoutrements that can be worn alone or together for a stronger his-for-her impression. There are many types of masculine looks, each with its own set of meanings, each expressing different aspects of a woman's personality. Some male-inspired clothing bespeaks a classical refinement, while other styles send messages of personal power or "machismo."

It is important to differentiate between a masculine look and one that is androgynous. Androgyny, in popular cultural terms, means wearing styles that convey ambiguous gender characteristics—a sort of melding of masculine and feminine that effectively obscures the wearer's sex. Donning androgynous apparel is a way of saying "I don't care to compete either with other women or with men. I'd rather that gender and sexuality not play a part in my overall appearance." Interestingly, the androgynous look comes across as both self-assured and nonchalant. Black clunky shoes, sweatshirts, oversize pants with suspenders, and cropped hair are all emblems of this particular style.

Unlike a woman impeccably attired in a man's three-piece suit, the androgynous dresser doesn't seek to mimic men's fashion; she transcends it. The appeal of androgyny is threefold:

1. It has a playful, ageless quality that makes the wearer appear more youthful.
2. It relieves the wearer of the need to either live up to the female ideal or compete with a masculine image. So she feels and appears relaxed and comfortable.
3. It projects an innocent eroticism based on the mysterious ambiguity about the wearer's sexuality.

THE SEX APPEAL OF LOOKING LIKE A MAN

As I've already mentioned, many men find the stark contrast of a woman in mannish clothing quite alluring. Masculine wear imbues a woman with bravado and self-assurance that is often expressed as a particular kind of sexiness. But the male-garbed woman may also appeal to men for other reasons—some that may be at cross purposes with her own goals. Her mannish appearance not only allows men to enjoy homosexual fantasies but serves to alleviate their fear of commitment, marriage, procreation—even castration.

The sight of a woman in men's clothing enables men to think of recreational sex as opposed to procreational sex—since intimacy with the same sex does not lead to babies. And because traditional rules pertaining to male/female relationships seem constraining or outmoded to some men, the sight of an "androgynous" woman shatters such conventions, making them feel more relaxed.

Then there is the sexual feeling *women* get from wearing men's fashions. How many of us have raided our husband's, boyfriend's, or father's closets? Worn and slept in their shirts? When we need something special to complete an outfit, haven't we been known to borrow his tie or cap or jacket? Sometimes large masculine clothing simply makes us feel warm and protected, but wearing our daddy's, husband's, or boyfriend's clothes has another meaning as well. When we are literally *in his pants,* inside his clothes, it is like being in his embrace. We wrap ourselves in his masculinity, his sexuality—and feel turned on and protected by it at the same time.

THE TIE AS PHALLIC SYMBOL

The tie may be the most potent symbol of virility in that it represents an upside-down phallus. It's no wonder that men feel "incomplete" without the suit's mandatory accessory.

Prior to the mid-nineteenth century, scarves or cravats were worn wrapped loosely around the neck. But at midcentury the progenitor of the modern-day tie appeared. It was tied either in a bow or in a ball-like knot at the neck, with the remainder hanging down to the middle of the chest, the latter even more strongly evocative of the male genitals than contemporary incarnations.

Like most other fashion accessories, ties can be elegant, whimsical, sporty, formal, or artistic. As for its "maleness," a skinny string tie conveys a less virile image than a broader tie; a coarse fabric is more masculine than a smooth one; a geometric pattern is more macho than a floral.

Many men rebel against wearing a tie at all—perceiving them to be as restrictive as high heels or tight skirts are for women. Perhaps because we are not in fact required to wear one, women are more appreciative of a mannish tie and the "put-together" look it brings to a tailored or sporty outfit. This, of course, in addition to the potency implicit in its phallic characteristics!

A man's reaction to seeing a woman in a tie varies, depending on his point of view. While some men might feel threatened, others see the style as a welcome emblem of equality. An unconventional man might perceive a tie-clad woman as a willing victim of a dress code he rejects, while another finds the look cute and sexy.

THE BANKER LOOK

Because they are associated with lawyers, bankers, and other professionals, mannish double-breasted suits with pinstripes and exaggerated shoulders denote high economic standing and social prestige.

The array of garments available to women to create this illusion is vast: a few examples include the crisp white shirt, suspenders, thin neckties, thick-soled oxfords, vests with fobs, double-breasted jackets, and Calvary tweed jackets in expensive fabrics. Such items help us appear more accomplished and more powerful than a more traditionally feminine suit. And seeing our feminine persona outfitted in apparel reflective of male success has an arresting effect on co-workers.

However, there is also a sinister side to this particular characterization of the male, since it signifies traits some find morally reprehensible—such as the unscrupulous financial manipulator; the cold, unfeeling businessman personified by Michael Douglas in the film *Wall Street.* Along with the social stature is a suggestion of aggression and cruelty; isn't greed, after all, an essential ingredient in obtaining the success this look signifies?

Still, the particular status and magnetism implicit in the conservative banker look appeals to many women who wish to appear forceful and commanding.

DANDYISM

Dandyism in men is a refined and slightly eccentric passion for beauty represented by sartorial splendor and exquisite clothing. Signifying a yearning for a more civilized culture, dandyism found significant expression in the nineteenth century. The dandy of that era was dedicated to external perfection; personified by such celebrities as Oscar Wilde and Marcel Proust, the dandyistic aesthetic consisted of artistic chic manifested in creative, opulent clothing.

The modern dandy revels in differentiating himself from society and liberating himself from its dictates. His aim is to achieve perfection and self-assurance and to bring form and style to a world that is falling apart. Baudelaire put it most succinctly when he said, "For the true dandy, the perfection of personal appearance consists in complete simplicity—this being in fact the best means of achieving distinction." The dandy wants to be known for his or her individuality.

However, while male dandies risk appearing foppish and being thought frivolous, self-indulgent, or even silly, the woman as dandy comes across as a stylish rebel: original, artistic, feminine, and clever. Edwardian details such as velvet jackets, lace collars, and turned-back cuffs are integral to the dandy look, as are tight-fitting waistcoats and trousers. Rich fabrics are also a must, and accessories often have phallic overtones. Black or white dinner jackets with silk or satin trim; elegant tuxedos, replete with vest, walking stick, and top hat; capes lined in satin; baggy trousers; big jackets with shoulder pads; gold cuff links; watch fobs; bowlers; and black patent-leather shoes are all found in a dandy's wardrobe. Think of Julie Andrews in *Victor/Victoria.*

THE WOMAN IN UNIFORM

One year, Ralph Lauren sent models down the runway in military naval outfits, overt references to combat and military power. An entourage of gorgeous female soldiers strutting menacingly in unison in their Eisenhower jackets—which resembled West Point cadet jackets with their wide, military capes—were particularly arresting.

All such fashions send a not-so-subtle message to women: "Wear these clothes and you, too, shall feel powerful."

The military uniform is one of the most forceful symbols of strength and potency a woman can wear. It proclaims both authority and cooperation. Stylish spin-offs of naval officers' and police uniforms have all made their way to the couture houses, transforming function into fashion.

A less refined and perhaps less alloyed way to convey this same message, authentic military wear has long been popular with both sexes, beginning in the 1960s when antiwar activists donned army garb and adorned themselves with military paraphernalia in an ironic protest against the war in Vietnam. Wearing the uniforms of America's military forces in such a casual manner showed an intentional disdain and lack of respect for the military and political leadership of that era.

Today, wearing fashionable military garb may not have such strong political significance, but it has a definite psychological connotation. Since military and naval uniforms emphasize the chest and shoulders, these desirable masculine aspects are part of their appeal. Military-inspired hats clearly draw attention to bold-featured faces; cuffed pants show off the aggressive, large, chunky shoes that are de rigueur for this look; and shiny brass buttons demand recognition and respect.

SHIRKING THE BAGGAGE OF FEMININITY

We reveal our motives for adopting androgynous dress through the styles we select. Certain elements announce our values and our vision of ourselves. We've referred to the unique appeal of the dandy, the banker, and the soldier. Following are additional masculine-inspired looks.

THE BRAWN LOOK

Dressing in tight, muscle-clinging T-shirts, tight jeans, and motorcycle jackets à la Marlon Brando or James Dean, is a way of suggesting that we are competing for the physical prowess previously achieved only by men. Actually this brand of androgyny may express the need for a third sex: the exquisite combination of male and female strengths.

THE MODERN-DAY ROBIN HOOD LOOK

On the other end of the androgynous spectrum is the miniskirt or tunic with leggings or tights, a style strikingly similar to that worn by men in the fifteenth century. Those who dress in this fashion usually want to create a sense of ambiguity or multifacetedness.

THE MACHO LOOK

The adoption of heavy metal chains and belts, clunky boots (cowboy or biker), oversize leather jackets with huge zippers, leather pants, and a total lack of anything that looks remotely feminine may project a woman's fear of being associated with feminine attributes and come across as a sign of hostility to men.

THE SOCIALLY ACCEPTABLE UNISEX STYLE

The clean-cut form of androgyny represented by classic trousers, shirts, and sweaters of the variety found at the Gap or J. Crew proclaims our preference for comfort and simplicity. It's less about trying to make a statement than about paring down our clothing choices to straightforward, clean lines and easy-to-wear natural fabrics that shatter gender barriers. The woman who wears such garments conveys that she has less demanding expectations of people and is less likely to judge others according to sexual stereotypes. She tosses aside preconceived notions of what it means to be a woman or a man and values people for what they are rather than how they look.

MENSWEAR LOOKS AND MESSAGES

1. The Look
   ◆ Oversize man's blazer, pleated trousers, shirt, and long overcoat
   or
   ◆ Oversize man-tailored shirt, big blazer, and jeans

The Message
- I'm a little girl dressed in my father's clothes. Take care of me.

2. The Look
- Wool blazer, turtleneck, cashmere scarf, jeans, and oxfords

The Message
- I'm as sophisticated, intellectual, and elegant as any of my male counterparts

3. The Look
- Tweed suit with cashmere crewneck

The Message
- I can be stylish and have fun at the same time.

4. The Look
- Man-tailored suit over sweater, shirt, and tie

The Message
- My preppie days served me well.

5. The Look
- Man-tailored suit and tie, with no female embellishments

The Message
- I can compete with any man—even if I do have to try harder.

6. The Look
- Black leather jacket with biker boots

The Message
- I want to be more powerful, like one of the guys.

7. The Look
- Black leather jacket over cashmere sweater

The Message
- I'm strong but soft at the same time.

8. The Look
- Pants with men's suspenders

The Message
- I feel like an old-fashioned schoolboy.

9. The Look
- Cowboy jacket or peacoat, jeans, and boots

The Message
- I'm gregarious, rugged, down-to-earth.

C h a p t e r 5

Dress Code on the Job: What Works and Why

"He who has nothing to assert has no style and can have none."

—*G. B. Shaw*

A woman, a journalist assigned to interview a Nobel Prize-winning author, is standing in front of her closet in her bathrobe—her contact lenses in, her makeup on—frantically searching for something to wear. The phone rings. It's her boyfriend. "Wear your red suit," he says.

"Too bright," she answers.

"Well then, your navy-blue jumpsuit."

"Not dressy enough."

"How about that black knit skirt?"

"Too sexy."

"Well," he says, and she can hear in his voice the effort it's taking him not to lose his patience, "how do you want to look?"

"Intelligent," she answers.

"Wear your glasses," he tells her. (Taken from *The New Yorker*, August 1989)

As dozens of books and magazines devoted to "dressing for success" attest, the clothes, the makeup, and the accessories you wear to work can help present a strong professional image and positively influence your business interactions. Knowing that the clothing you've selected supports and reinforces the impression you hope to create will make you feel more confident and more able to assert yourself. However, dressing "appropriately" is only half the battle.

By tailoring your wardrobe to fit the image you want to project in the workplace, you can send your superiors and colleagues strong messages about your ambition, team spirit, creativity, and enthusiasm. Depending on your career goals, you may want to blend seamlessly into the corporate gestalt, or you may prefer to cut a higher profile, identifying yourself as an individualist who breaks rather than lives by the rules. You don't need to show up for work in a flaming red cocktail dress to proclaim yourself an individualist, however; these messages can—and should—be far more subtle and fall within the bounds of what is fitting and acceptable in your own profession. There is certainly merit to the notion of fitting into your surroundings, showing that you are a team player who knows the company rules and can adopt the team colors with grace and ease; but often, in doing so, you risk losing your sense of personal identity. The trick is in finding a balance between fitting in and revealing your uniqueness.

Continuity in dress is also important in business. Taking on a different style or image each week says the wearer is unstable, indecisive. If she cannot settle on her style, she will not be able to make grounded decisions. Why should a colleague take her seriously when she herself is likely to take a new point of view?

When they reach the top of their fields, women feel freer to dress as they please. The woman with a distinct personal style has established her own uniform. She is often too busy with creative endeavors to worry about the vagaries of fashion. She knows what she wants and what she likes, and she sticks with it, adding a few carefully chosen pieces to her wardrobe each year to keep it up-to-date.

Of course, even these loose strictures have undergone enormous change over the last few decades, as the pendulum concerning appropriate work clothing for women has swung back and forth between feminine looks and those that mimic the masculine. The wide-shouldered look is a not-so-subtle stylized echo of the male physique. In a garment with added dimension in the shoulder area, women naturally feel stronger, more powerful, more commanding. Although the ultratailored "menswear" look remains a strong component of a successful business wardrobe, it is no longer necessary for a woman to dress like her male colleagues to prove she is their equal.

Shoulder pads for women were first ushered in in the 1940s, an era of increasing female presence in the workplace, as women were called upon to fill positions once occupied by men who had gone off to war. It's no wonder the style was popular then. The shoulder pad faded in the fifties when women were displaced from the workforce and resumed a more domestic role, but it made a comeback in the early eighties as women began making strides in the workplace.

As we head into the twenty-first century, the once obligatory-for-business shoulder pad is no longer the unquestioned standard—nor are we satisfied to accept other widely held notions of what makes a woman appear powerful. We are beginning to realize just how potent the female silhouette is on its own.

Whereas once we needed to mimic the masculine in order to appear authoritative and assertive, we've now earned the right to look more feminine by proving our capability in the working world. The natural shape of a woman's legs, waist, and bosom are replacing artificially wide shoulders as respectable indicators of competence. It's no longer a fashion sin for a woman to look like a woman in her place of business.

Although the modified shoulder pad look continues to be popular—giving the illusion of dominance while whittling down the waists and slenderizing the hips—designers are now eschewing the male look-alike clothing aesthetic for career styles that accentuate a woman's contours. Soft, rounded shoulders; suits and jackets with softer lines and delicate feminine detail; and nipped-in waists, flared skirts, and peplums are all popular. The bottom line is that we now have more freedom to determine how we want to look at work. And knowing how you want to be perceived is the first thing to consider.

Start by recognizing that the so-called dress-for-success uniform is far from being a safe or foolproof choice. While you may generally feel more comfortable in such a traditional, "conformist" outfit, this look could imply to others that your ideas are conventional as well. Although ideal for certain management positions, in a creative atmosphere where originality is a crucial requisite for success, it could dampen your chances for advancement.

In the strictly codified world of the bottom and lower rungs of the corporate ladder, most women feel safest adhering to the stringent rules of traditional business dress. However, once you're well on your way to achieving your goals, you will want to dress in a style that reflects the confidence you feel in your accomplishments. If you cling to the old dress-for-success code, you will most likely come across as insecure; others will assume you are uncertain of your own personality and unable or afraid to initiate new ideas or explore new territory. And interestingly enough, such restrictive fashion choices may actually restrict your receptivity to other kinds of innovation as well.

In fact, it has been shown that creative dressers are more open to new ideas than those who dress conservatively. In a study done by John Summers, over one thousand women were asked about their lives, details of their personalities and attitudes, how often they talked about fashion, and how often others asked their advice on clothing. He found that those with an individual sense of fashion were also highly educated, extroverted, and possessed of high self-esteem. His findings also concluded that fashion innovators were well liked, emotionally stable, and confident. Independent dress signifies a woman who is sure enough of herself to form her own opinions and be open to the ideas of others.

FIRST MEETINGS: HOW CLOTHING INFLUENCES BUSINESS INTERACTIONS

Sherry is a thirty-five-year-old divorced mother of two and vice president of a top cosmetics firm. She very deliberately cultivates an ultrafeminine image in order to counterbalance her tough negotiating style. The day we spoke, she looked beautifully serene in a pale pink suit and lace blouse, her face framed with soft curls. "Don't be deceived," she told me with a wink. "I'm as shrewd and calculating as the next guy—maybe more so. But I use my appearance to reassure business associates that I'm not as aggressive as I sometimes act."

It should go without saying that clothing is as important a part of making a good business impression as a firm handshake or carefully plotted chart. At every meeting your colleagues will assess your appearance and demeanor. Your clothing is a shorthand but very effective way to convey your business personality and for those determining your intentions to come to a favorable conclusion.

When dressing for a business meeting, consider whom you will meet. If you're the editor-in-chief of a magazine, you might wear casual attire—such as a turtleneck, leggings, boots, and a blazer—when meeting with writers and photographers. However, you would definitely wear a suit when meeting with the board of directors. If you wore the suit with the creative people, it might make them uncomfortable, just as the free-spirited garb would not sit well with executives, who want to know that their money and trust rest in responsible—in other words, conventional—hands.

As your business look evolves, make sure that it's flexible enough to allow room for variations; no look, when adhered to rigidly, will be appropriate for every business occasion. Fortunately this doesn't mean you must have the equivalent of a department store in your closet. Often it is the simple yet telling details of our clothing that carry the most potent messages.

SUITS AND JACKET

Even if your job requires you to rely on a basic wardrobe of suits or jackets, don't feel this eliminates the opportunity to send a message about yourself. The texture and tone of a suit fabric, the stiffness of a shirt, and the proportions of a skirt and jacket are all reliable indicators of the wearer's personal business style. The woman who arrives at a meeting in a low-cut, soft wool crepe jacket will come across as more flexible than the one wearing a stiff gabardine jacket. A buttoned-up suit may make you feel protected and efficient, but it also sends a message that you're guarded. Rigid, starched, pointed collars (especially when buttoned up) usually reflect an uncompromising style.

People tend to feel more secure around a woman in a loosely constructed suit. Instinctively they feel she's more open and easygoing, and this puts them at ease. If you choose a stiff, navy blue or black suit, you may state your authority, but you could also appear uncompromising. The rigidity of the fabric suggests an inflexible temperament, and the dark color indicates a private nature—a woman who is not very willing to reveal her thoughts immediately. If you choose to wear a lightweight fabric (like cashmere or silk) in light or bright tones, such as fuchsia or red, you will bring life to a business meeting. This kind of outfit indicates that there is nothing somber about the way you think, that you're not afraid to experiment with new fashion colors—or new ideas.

COLLAR SHAPES

What you wear under a suit says as much about you as the suit itself:

◆ An unbuttoned collar indicates an open-minded, flexible woman.

◆ A crumpled, floppy collar proclaims incompetence.

◆ Loose collars reflect a casual person, one who may be slack in her work. This message is especially strong when such a collar is worn by women in managerial positions.

◆ Shirts with pointed, angular, or oddly shaped collars indicate a highly creative individual whose thoughts and ideas are anything but conventional.

◆ A huge, dramatic collar shows an authoritative person with a powerful and dynamic personality.

◆ A blouse with a small Peter Pan collar detracts from authority because its presence is so tentative. (This collar is associated with children's clothing and was named after the character who didn't want to grow up.)

The Ups and Downs of Hemlines

Skirt length is an equally good indicator of a woman's personal business style. When choosing the best skirt length for the office, you should look at a number of other considerations beyond what the fashion magazines have decreed as the "in" length of the season.

For example, someone in a long, slim skirt is seen as sophisticated but somewhat aloof. Because length and narrowness restrict movement, they imply the wearer may have a restricted or contained point of view. While long, narrow skirts can make a woman appear standoffish, the wide expanse of a long, full skirt makes her seem warmer and more approachable. These skirts are open and fluid; their fullness allows for greater movement of the legs, and this freedom of movement makes the wearer appear open and easygoing.

While long, narrow skirts imply sophistication, short skirts look more youthful, suggesting an open, spirited, and vigorous mind—a strong, creative person. Short, pleated skirts that swing allude to a more easygoing nature than do tight skirts. The fluidity of the skirt reflects a lively personality. But though a woman wearing a short, full skirt may appear younger at heart, she may also come off less mature. A long jacket or sweater over a short skirt adds sophistication to a youthful, spontaneous look. The same over a short pleated skirt offers an even friendlier image.

Dress Code Violations
in the Workplace

Of course, the more obvious dress code violation, such as charm bracelets, long dangling earrings, or four-inch heels, spell doom in conservative professions. But there are a number of less obvious ways in which women unknowingly sabotage themselves in the workplace through their attire. Such wardrobe mistakes can be costly.

DRESS CODE

A woman in a predominantly male firm who shows up in ruffles or flowered prints may become subconsciously associated with passivity and dependence in the minds of her co-workers; thus her suggestions may be overlooked or she may be overruled on decisions or passed over for higher assignments. The woman who presents a girlish image may elicit parental or authoritative reactions; wearing lace, florals, crochet, or whimsical clothing to a business meeting can be especially detrimental if she hopes to sway opinions or propose an unconventional strategy, as these looks are associated with sweetness and youthfulness, not strength.

There is a fine line between appropriate and inappropriate workplace attire—a line that is often crossed. For example, a woman may feel that by wearing expensive, extravagant clothing, she projects an image of power. Sadly, this couldn't be farther from the truth. Showy, ostentatious clothing does not impress or intimidate business associates; rather, it signals to others that the wearer is not serious about her work. Such displays of conspicuous consumption should be confined to the social arena.

"It is not that the dress is wrong. It is the fact that the dress is worn at the wrong time or the wrong place. It is a sense of timing."—Oscar de la Renta

---

Being adequately yet not overly covered is an important part of looking competent, especially in business. Studies show that women who dress in layers—such as a blouse topped by a blazer—are viewed as more authoritative than those who wear only one garment, such as a dress. Covering the skin with only a single thin layer suggests vulnerability.

DRESSED FOR FAILURE

Certain looks or styles, rather than supporting the image you hope to project, undermine you before you've even had a chance to open your mouth. They do not encourage those you meet to take you seriously or treat you with respect, because they signify a lack of those very qualities within yourself. When you dress in an overtly sexual manner, for example, you undercut your own authority, deemphasizing those qualities that colleagues respect: intelligence, expertise, and trustworthiness. Provocative clothing may make you feel empowered and sensual in social settings, but they will elicit entirely different responses in the office. Dressing sexy suggests you don't have confidence in your work and ideas and need to employ sexual wiles to win battles.

The woman who wants to complete the deal and direct the negotiations should *not*

◆ wear anything that reveals cleavage.

- go braless.

- wear skirts too short to allow her to sit down without fear of revealing too much.

- wear transparent or lace fabrics or strapless tops.

On the other hand, you also undercut your image when you turn out in drab, nondescript clothing. Such clothing might be considered "invisible," but in fact it elicits a negative rather than a neutral response. Examples include faded blazers, khaki skirts, or frumpy, outdated suits. Clothes that say "Don't look at me" or "I don't care" usually reveal low self-esteem. Wearing them conveys that we don't feel worthy of respect, aren't entitled to look good, and are uncomfortable wielding power. By wearing clothing that will elicit negative responses, we set ourselves up for failure.

Less overt but just as telling to outside observers is a mismatched style: wearing a tailored jacket with a feminine, flowered skirt or throwing a leather motorcycle jacket over a business suit. Such ambivalence may indicate a sense of disorientedness and disorganization in the woman who wears them.

Overly frivolous garments or accessories undermine a woman's professionalism and cast doubt on the soundness of her decision-making abilities. Others will fear that if she cannot choose her clothing wisely, she will exercise bad judgment in professional situations as well.

UNSPOKEN DRESS CODES FOR PROFESSIONS

It is always better to be perceived as an independent thinker than as a conformist who blindly follows the pack. But your fashion individuality should be tempered by the accepted norms of your profession. All else being equal, the woman who conforms to the dress code of the particular industry she's in is likely to get promoted over someone who does not. Every profession adheres to a code, although in few offices is it ever delineated explicitly. Conservative fields such as government, banking, insurance, and law set strict demarcations for appropriate dress and expect employees to stay within those boundaries. Creative fields such as media, advertising, publishing, and the arts allow (and even expect) a higher degree of individuality and innovation. Regardless of where your workplace is situated on the fashion spectrum, it's important to be mindful of the rules.

Different professions require different fashion approaches. Shelley S. Harp, Shirley Stretch, and Dennis A. Harp at the University of Texas studied the effect dress has on a woman's career and how she is perceived. They used the television news anchorwoman as their subject and found that clothing affected how reliable she was perceived by viewers.

Not surprising, their study showed that a proper, conservative appearance lent an aura of credibility to newspeople that a more flamboyant outfit did not. It's not hard to understand that an understated style is most effective for delivering news about war and natural disasters or that a more colorful, whimsical outfit would be fine for hosting an entertainment program.

Working Woman magazine did an unscientific study of the different styles of clothing in offices. The article, entitled "Grooming and Other Rituals of the Modern Workplace," showed how unwritten dress codes vary from industry to industry and company to company.

◆ At Lazard Freres and Co., an investment banking corporation, the only acceptable skirt length was just above the knee, and pants were not allowed. Light lipstick and pearl earrings were acceptable, shoes were flat or high, depending on a woman's preference.

◆ On the other end of the spectrum, at CBS Entertainment in Los

Angeles, the most commonly worn skirt length was several inches above the knee. Female employees complemented their outfits with bold accessories, flats, opaque tights, and long, loose hairstyles. Pants were worn widely, as were jeans.

◆ At the Calvin Klein company, employees wore what Calvin designed. Minimal accessories, well-cut hair, natural makeup, and pants were encouraged.

◆ At Skadden, Arps, Slate, Meagher & Flom, a large New York law firm, miniskirts to midlengths, big bracelets, midheight heels, and shoulder-length hair were the code. Partners wore pants with high heels.

◆ At N. W. Ayers and Co., an advertising agency in New York City, dress was quite different for the creative and account people. While the account people wore suits with gold buttons, clip-on earrings, heels, and prominent lipstick, the creative people wore denim skirts and T-shirts or jeans with jackets, dangling earrings, flat shoes, and little makeup.

Mastering the unspoken dress code of your particular corporation or industry can help you project a professional demeanor as long as you don't subscribe to it *too* rigidly.

Following are some rules of thumb.

LAW, BANKING, INSURANCE, AND OTHER CONSERVATIVE PROFESSIONS

Clients may well assess their lawyer's capability based on her image. Thus female attorneys need to apply the same balanced judgment to choosing their clothes that they do to putting together a case. Such attention to one's appearance will instill trust not only in clients but in co-workers as well.

Suits are still the most appropriate "uniform" for those of you who work in a conservative profession. You'll need to select outfits that project a sense of authority and competence, keeping in mind that in informal meetings with clients, your style should be more relaxed than it needs to be in the boardroom or courtroom. Unbuttoning your top shirt button or jacket is a simple way to "unstuff" the room and help break the ice.

A business suit can still be femininely tailored and have a personalized flair, dash, and panache. A nontraditional yet well-cut suit in an unexpected color can be a refreshing change yet still project a professional air. It should not, however, deviate widely from the implicit or explicit dress code.

A commanding suit in a flattering color, a good watch, a feminine yet professional briefcase, pearls, and antique gold pins are all ways to spruce up a conservative outfit. And using accessories to express personal style reveals that you're willing to take some chances—even the most conservative professions value insight and originality as highly as they do stolid reliability.

Minimal makeup and jewelry also can convey authority. It suggests that you don't need accoutrements—that you are secure and confident enough to remain understated and still command respect. Just be certain that your overall look isn't drab or dated, as this can communicate a sense of stagnation.

In conservative fields, skirts should not go any higher than the top of the knee, and low to midheel shoes are mandatory. Flats are too arty, and high heels are too sexy. Scarves and pocket squares add a dash of color, and good watches, subtle jewelry in gold, and pearls also work well to enliven a business outfit. Bold prints or tiny floral print dresses do *not* work in the ultraconservative professions, however. These items lack power and prestige. Anything provocative is out, so avoid sheer fabrics; short, tight skirts; armloads of bangles; or dangling earrings.

DRESS CODE

SALES AND MARKETING

Women who work in sales and marketing are in contact with clients on a daily basis. As representatives of their company and products, they must wear garments that put others at ease yet still have a dash of panache.

If you're in sales, your objective is to leave a lasting impression—and many women are smart enough to employ their wardrobes in that effort. An understated jacket, separates, or unmatched suits often work better than matched suits because they imply that you're comfortable with your own personal style and don't need anyone to make choices for you. Subtly rich fabrics and fine tailoring convey that the individual and her company are of the finest quality as well.

HELPING PROFESSIONS

In the "helping professions," such as teaching, health care, and counseling, comfortable clothes are very important. Take pains to look relaxed and open, not aloof or forbidding. Your clothes should communicate "I am not going to judge, intimidate, or hurt you. I am a person just like you, who can understand your concerns." Such clothes allow a lot of room for individuality. For example, ethnic designs or interesting jewelry would reveal something of a therapist's personality and encourage her clients to open up. Since making a patient, client, or student feel at ease is critical, those in the helping professions should avoid overly tailored outfits and instead wear soft fabrics and soothing colors. Jackets should be loosely structured. An authoritative look may interfere with developing trust and rapport. Stiff collars inspire mistrust, while trendy clothes and high style tend to intimidate.

Teachers should also know that cheerful colors stimulate and bring life to a classroom. Vivid, bold, uplifting styles, low-heeled shoes, sweaters, and roomy skirts are good choices for those working with young children. Cardigan sweaters and trousers also work well.

THE JOB INTERVIEW

Interviewers observe a job applicant as keenly as a laboratory specimen. How we dress for an interview may reveal things about us we never realized. Our clothes not only introduce us, they also convey to others how we like to see ourselves. When dressing for an interview, we should choose clothing that articulates our personality as well as an understanding of what the job entails. When we want others to see us as creative and energetic, we should select an outfit distinct from the one we'd wear if we wanted to be remembered as intellectual, trustworthy, and reliable.

Learning to dress appropriately for an interview is so important, it ought to be a required course at every university. Consider two women of equal background and experience applying for an executive-level job at a large public relations firm. Because of the importance of this particular position, the firm has brought in an interviewer with a psychology degree to assess the candidates' overall qualities—above and beyond what is contained in their résumés.

The applicants' clothing is one important factor the interviewer will use as an indicator of how each would handle the job.

The first woman arrives in an impeccably tailored suit in exquisite navy blue wool crepe. Her skirt is conservative, hitting right above the knee. The collar of her white silk shirt crosses and buttons on opposite sides. She has affixed an elegant pin to the lapel of the jacket and wears matching earrings. On her feet are low-heeled Ferragamo pumps.

The next applicant has wrapped herself in a cloud of color. She wears a bouclé jacket in swirls of raspberry and pinks. The jacket is nipped at the waist and tops a soft pink merino wool skirt. A matching shawl is flung artfully across her shoulders.

Who got the job? According to the interviewer, the second woman triumphed over the first. Through her dress, she showed that she would approach the position with creativity and style, attributes highly prized in her chosen line of work. The interviewer pointed out that the first woman's suit was clearly of excellent quality, but her careful, conservative look betrayed a fear of asserting her own personal style.

While the first woman didn't display the imaginative flair needed for the public relations position, she could well have been hired over the other candidate for a management position because she exuded an aura of reliability. If she had been applying for a job in a financial institution, she would have also made an excellent impression. But an overly conservative look in creative fields is as jarring as creative styles are in conservative businesses and professions.

But even in a creative occupation, fashionable flair can sometimes send the wrong signals. The editor of a large Chicago paper was interviewing prospective reporters in training for the "Style" section. One interviewee arrived in a trendy outfit. As she took in the harried air and messy surroundings of the newsroom, she soon realized she had seriously miscalculated. Her frivolous, expensive clothing betrayed the fact that she had little sense of what kind of work this "glamorous" job entailed.

This message was confirmed during her interview, as the editor felt "she was communicating through her clothing that she really was not serious about learning reporting but was more interested in the perks and prestige of the job. She appeared more concerned with couture than with learning how to write good copy."

Sandra Forsythe at the University of Georgia and Mary Francis and Charles Cox at the University of Tennessee examined how an interviewee's dress influences her chances of being hired. Personnel officers viewed videotape of four interviewees in various outfits, all vying for the same management position.

The first woman wore a light beige dress in a soft fabric. The dress had a small, round collar, gathered skirt, and long sleeves. The second candidate wore a bright aqua suit with a short belted jacket and a white blouse with a large, softly draped bow at the neck. The third applicant wore a beige tailored suit with a blazer jacket and a rust blouse with a bow at the neck. The final woman wore a dark navy suit and white blouse with an angular collar.

The study showed that the more masculine and conservative the outfit, the stronger the hiring recommendations—up to a point. The most masculine suit received less favorable responses. In management, a conservative look is appropriate and expected, but trying to dress "like a man" can undermine a woman's credibility. Again, a woman will appear businesslike and less emotional in a tailored, mannish-style suit, but also less sensitive and creative. Softer, more feminine lines that physically define us as women can be a definite asset.

In an interview, your prospective employer will be trying to visualize you in the position for which you're applying, how you'll fit in and what you'll bring to the office mix. If your outfit is distracting, inappropriate, unkempt, or ill-fitting, it will definitely work against you. Know the appropriate dress at the job for which you're applying and then wear an upscale version of the clothing required.

In this way the interviewer will see a polished person who understands the position and its requirements. Consider these common interview wardrobe mistakes:

Dress Code Violation	Effect
uncoordinated outfits, clashing colors	make you appear disorganized and unprofessional
ill-fitting clothes that pull	distracting and unprofessional; show poor sense of self— don't know your own body flaws
poor grooming, including ragged fingernails, blotched makeup, or unkempt hair	reveals someone who doesn't pay attention to details, is sloppy and careless
jeans or any item that looks overly sporty or casual	makes you appear as if you won't take the job seriously
sirenlike, provocative clothing, including sheer tops, halters, too short skirts	interviewer will wonder if you're trying to use your sexuality to get the job; also bespeaks lack of good judgment, lack of intelligence
clothing completely out of sync with implicit industry dress codes and protocols	says you're naive about the necessity of playing by the rules
too much makeup	unbusinesslike; shows lack of judgment
extravagant evening-wear fabrics	indicates that you're unaware of what the position involves

Dress Code Violation	Effect
oversize, overstated, or very expensive jewelry	distracting, unprofessional
vibrant red suits	too overpowering
overstuffed bags	make you look disorganized
conservative suits if your job objective is in a creative field	you'll appear too rigid and unimaginative for the job
funky, trendy clothing if your job objective is in a conservative field	you'll appear too frivolous, unable to take the position seriously
floral print skirts with tailored jackets	mixed metaphor; you'll convey a scattered, disorderly quality
frills, ruffles, or any clothing with an adolescent quality	undermines your image of a mature, competent professional

Whether the context is business or social, clothes can never *make* the woman, but dressing the part gives you a distinct edge. In today's competitive business environment, you need to use every advantage available—and fashion can provide that advantage. In looking your best, expressing who you are, and at the same time adhering to the implicit dress codes of your chosen field, you're giving yourself the best shot at success. When you sensitively tailor your image to suit the professional setting in which you work, you not only feel more confident—which improves both your performance and your working relationships—you also enhance your chances of commanding the respect and trust you deserve. While the proper image is obviously no substitute for working hard or having creative ideas, it's too potent a force to ignore.

Fashion and Status: Under the Spell of Haute Couture

"To improve one's style means to improve one's thoughts and nothing else: He who does not admit this immediately will never be convinced of it."

—*Nietzsche*

WOULD YOU BE SEEN IN THIS OUTFIT? dares a headline in *Vogue* magazine. Accompanying the question are photographs of two models: one wears a shiny gold dress whose puffed-out petals portray her as a flower ripe for plucking; the other, in an outfit complete with breast cutouts and heavy silver zippers, appears to be a victim of medieval torture.

The designers who conceive these avant-garde spectacles are well aware of the impact they make. Fashion runways are showcases for designers' artistic visions and help inject new ideas into the industry. Many of the more outlandish outfits are there primarily for publicity purposes; the shows in which they appear are theatrical productions staged for the benefit of editors, buyers, and private clients, a way to provide the fashion media with fresh, colorful copy. Quite simply, they are not created for consumers and will in all likelihood never make it to the racks of local department stores. Buyers or fashion directors may find one or two pieces out of the hundreds that come down the runway that can be modified into a wearable item, but those are the exceptions, not the rule.

If you've ever scanned the pages of industry publications and felt hopelessly out of the fashion swing, don't despair. Most of us find little common ground between these eccentric displays of fashion "art" and what's hanging in our closet.

The fashion world is a subculture unto itself. Several of the outrageous designs that it foists upon an impressionable public can be laughable, vulgar, even disturbing. Shows held in such obscure locales as circuses, garbage dumps, or subway stations more closely resemble theater than a serious attempt to sell the average woman her wardrobe for next season. Ultimately, however, all but the most bizarre visions of haute couture do filter down to the masses in a diluted form.

> *"Women express themselves by their choice of accessories or clothing. But sometimes this choice is contrary to the way they are or the way they think. It's common to see a timid, shy woman wearing extravagant things, things that do not correspond to her personality. But it is her way of overcoming her fear."—Sonia Rykiel*

In 1968, for example, Yves Saint Laurent, who remains one of the world's most talented and influential designers, found inspiration in the social upheaval of the day and created "the happy whore look," a garish conglomeration of gargantuan shoulders, skimpy skirts, wild frizzled hairdos, and loud makeup. Not a particularly attractive image, but one that nonetheless found its way to Seventh

Avenue, where the cosmetic industry dumped their demure pastels in favor of bright red lipsticks and "whorish" rouge.

There are women, however, who buy their wardrobe based entirely on runway trends. When attention to trends overtakes good sense or even good taste, a fashion consumer can all too easily become a fashion victim.

Oscar de la Renta and John Fairchild coined the term *fashion victim* over lunch one afternoon. A fashion victim or fashion slave is someone who lets her clothing eclipse her personality. Such women are dealing subconsciously with issues of envy, competition, sexual insecurity, and low self-esteem.

Fashion slavery is characterized by a fear of individuality, the inability to trust one's own instincts, and the need to please, to be admired, noticed, or accepted. While it is true that some women dress audaciously as an artistic statement, others have more psychologically rooted reasons for wearing "cutting edge" fashion.

The fashion slave discounts comfort and suitability in favor of designer labels and the latest trend. If wide pants are in, she buys wide pants right away and wears them to the first function she can, even if that look is grossly incompatible with the occasion. If slim pants are in the next season, she'll throw out the wide ones, buy the skinny ones, and wear them at once—even if she's twenty pounds too heavy for this particular style and so uncomfortable in them that she can barely breathe!

Notoriety and the Fashion Slave

Fashion slaves often find themselves the target of Richard Blackwell, creator of the Worst Dressed list, who makes a living poking fun at everyone from the duchess of York to Dolly Parton. Nine out of ten women who appear on his list have worn what fashion dictates rather than clothing that represents their true personalities.

"Women should have their own image," the outspoken Mr. Blackwell says, "not become walking hangers for Seventh Avenue, which is basically what they are. They are so intimidated by the dictates of fashion that they're afraid to be 'out.' They wear what's 'in' to be recognized and resort to outrageous things to draw attention to themselves or become the 'innest' people in town. The only thing they are doing is making cartoons of themselves.

"A lot of women," he adds, "just need some tender loving care. If they got it, they might not have to resort to clothing tricks. Many just need to hear from their husbands, 'What a good dinner . . . what a great job of raising the kids you did. . . .' People are so afraid to love each other, to show anything that is obvious, that they feed another's need and subsequent quest for attention. This is what we are really missing."

FASHION SLAVERY—THE EMOTIONAL ISSUES

"There are very few women who are secure enough to look sophisticated and understated. I think one of the biggest mistakes women make in terms of their dress is that they have to show everything they own. A well-dressed woman does not have to depend on labels and fashion trends to look good."

—Isaac Mizrahi

When a woman becomes a slave to fashion, there is likely to be something lacking in her sense of self or identity. Afraid that if she does not conform to a certain stereotype she won't be accepted by her peers, she becomes preoccupied with her appearance and overly concerned with what other women think of her clothes, hairstyle, and jewelry. She may need a husband's or boyfriend's approval before purchasing any new article of clothing. Being "in fashion" is a way to assure herself that she is doing something right.

The ceaseless longing to be "in style" is really the desire to be validated. A fashion victim's concern isn't whether her clothes flatter her but rather that they be "au courant." Fashion slaves who must rush out to buy the newest fad are afraid to be creative. Trying anything outside the norm or expressing who they really are is simply too threatening.

Although many of us have difficulty accepting our bodies, viewing them as something to be "whipped into shape," fashion slaves take this tendency to an extreme. For the woman with wide hips and large breasts, the compulsive need to conform to the shape of a fashion model drives her to futile and inappropriate diets, extreme fitness routines, and emotional guilt trips. Rather than accepting her body, she dedicates herself to the pursuit of an unattainable image.

This compulsion to mimic an idealized cultural image is a throwback to adolescence, when it's normal to seek peer approval and strive to "fit in" with the group. At this stage of life, a young woman's identity and personality aren't yet fully developed, and her association with peers bolsters her sense of self. Unfortunately, many women remain emotionally underdeveloped even after they reach adulthood. They still desperately need outside approval, and being flawlessly "in fashion" seems a good way to win that.

FASHION GONE AWRY

Two things that are *not* vital to a fashion slave are comfort and looking appropriate. They are perfectly willing to sacrifice comfort for what they believe is "style" and lack the perspective to know when they look ridiculous.

Informing every proper fashion choice is the essential tenet that clothing must be suited to our age, coloring, and body type, as well as to the particular occasion. A flexible woman can indulge herself in a number of different styles and looks as long as she adheres to this basic principle.

Most of us have experienced feeling underdressed, overdressed, or just plain uncomfortable with what we've chosen to wear. But when one habitually dresses inappropriately, it may indicate underlying psychological issues—namely, a need for attention and approval so great that normal considerations of courtesy and decorum are ignored. Examples include the woman who attends a funeral in a brightly colored sundress, or wears a white extravaganza to a wedding—intentionally upstaging the bride.

As for the comfort issue, it seems obvious to most of us that when a woman spends half the day pulling her too short, too tight skirt down over her crotch, she shouldn't be wearing it in the first place. Wearing clothes that require constant attention simply does not make sense. A woman should feel at ease in her clothes. How can she feel attractive if her pants are one inch short of busting a button? In her compulsion to be fashionably correct, she succeeds only in looking silly and calling attention to her lack of good judgment.

THE FASHION SLAVE AS EXTREMIST

One characteristic common to all fashion victims is a need for control. Because she feels such fierce competitiveness when it comes to fashion, an extremist will leave a party if she encounters another woman wearing the same dress. Her need for control results in out-of-control behavior. Obsessed with her appearance, she spends much of her emotional energy on her clothing and too much of her money shopping. She must have her "shopping fix" habitually, regardless of the extent of her existing wardrobe.

The fashion extremist wears nothing for more than a season, and her clothes are so trendy, they're passé after only a few months of wear. Her clothing provides the only sense of self she may possess: an impeccably up-to-date wardrobe. Again, the underlying reason for fashion slavedom (extremists being one particular type) is a fundamental void that needs to be filled.

"To be overdressed, to be a victim of fashion or to follow fashion in such a way that all other aspects of her life are secondary, is an enormous mistake."—Valentino

Some women feel stuck in an uncreative job or a marriage that is not nourishing, so they look to their appearance to take up the slack. Purchasing becomes a nurturing experience. Every woman knows the momentary high buying something new offers. When it becomes obsessive, however, it may mean we aren't taking proper care of ourselves in other ways or getting enough nurturing from others.

There is a ruthlessness in the extremist's pursuit of fashion. Too much is never enough, and she doesn't think twice about sweeping through a boutique or department store, spending huge amounts of money in a matter of hours. She feels about shopping the way an alcoholic feels about a drink. Sometimes her sprees are triggered by a particular occasion or rationalization—such as a ski trip or a new job—but just as often they're brought on by emotional events.

PERSONAL CHANGE GOALS FOR THE EXTREMIST

For the extremist fashion slave, being "in fashion" is a profound need that dominates her life, often resulting in financial problems and interfering with family and personal relationships. But these are only symptoms of unresolved underlying issues.

Understand and accept that an unrelenting quest for the latest fashionable items is a search not to fill your closet but to fill a deeper void. Examine your life and try to determine what areas need attention. How can you derive more satisfaction from your work or your relationships? Are there conflicts that should be addressed?

Also, think about why you find yourself following fashion trends rather than trusting your own creative instincts. Perhaps those instincts need developing. Enroll in a jewelry or fashion design course. Learn how to sew, or take an art class to better understand shape and color, or a dance class to better appreciate the body, its form and movement. As you learn what attracts you and what interests you, you'll begin to enjoy who you are. In turn, you'll become better able to develop a style uniquely your own, and your need to "follow" will diminish.

WARDROBE GOALS FOR THE EXTREMIST

Understand that capitulating to every trend creates a lack of continuity in your wardrobe. Try buying classic styles and more accessories. You'll find that less truly is more. Each season make a checklist of what you need to give your wardrobe a lift. Take action to curb impulsive spending.

Take your credit cards out of your wallet, and if you find something you feel you can't live without, ask the salesperson to hold it for an hour or a day. Go home and examine your closet (and your bank account) to determine how the new "must have" works with what you already have. Plan ahead, and take pride in the longevity of your style rather than caving in to every fleeting fad.

ARE YOU A FASHION EXTREMIST?

How many of these items lurk in your closet?

◆ Gold lamé water holster from Gucci

◆ Black leather beeper cases and cellular phone cases disguised as evening bags

◆ Gold sequin, metallic, or jeweled baseball caps

◆ Folding Jean Paul Gaultier sunglasses and lipstick bracelets

---

- Hervé Leger bandage dresses

- Fishnet stockings

- Mambo clothing with big frothy skirts

- Over-the-thigh leather or velvet boots

- Patent-leather skirts

- Red sequin evening gown

- Thierry Mugler sequin catsuit

- Tartan leggings and blazers

- Thongs and cropped Lycra tanks that show off a well-flattened abdomen

- Belts that show off a streamlined waist

- Exaggerated seventies-inspired platform shoes

- Bondage-inspired evening clothes from Dolce & Gabbana and Jean Paul Gaultier

- Anything from Jean Paul Gaultier's newest collection

- Thierry Mugler suits (preferably with a nest of feathers around the neck and vinyl cuffs)

- Thick-soled shoes or sinister black leather boots

- Leather bustiers

- Dramatic hats

- Issey Miyake pleated extravaganzas

- Bandage and mummy Lycra dresses

- Azzedine Alaia dresses—the shorter and tighter, the better

- Pucci leggings

- Elaborately tooled cowboy boots or ten-gallon hats

And how many of these items can be found in or around your makeup table?

- False eyelashes

- Animal print makeup bags

- Status charm bracelets

- Colored contact lenses

- Purple lipstick

- Fake costume jewelry—too big, too much

- Lots of gold

THE STEPFORD WIFE

This breed of fashion slave is usually married to a wealthy, powerful man. Many have "married up," and money is new to them. Their lives are consumed by charity events, parties, and the couture, and they use image and beauty to catapult themselves up society's ever wobbly ladder. Having taken full advantage of their beauty and social cunning by marrying powerful, rich men, after their wedding day they erase their personal history and reinvent themselves according to the parameters of their husband's world.

The Stepford wife relies on clothing and makeup for her sense of well-being and is never caught without the "right" attire. She communicates largely through her appearance. Fixated on clothing, she expends much of her energy worrying about what to wear, and often she is critical of others who do not meet her own standards. Usually she does not work outside the home. Her life revolves around the beauty salon, fashion magazines, haute couture, parties, and shopping expeditions.

Her husband's role is of particular importance, as she often looks to him for validation and relates to him as the female image she so carefully constructs. She equates her husband's approval of her clothing with his acceptance of her and often asserts her desirability by dressing to annoy other women, wearing provocative, extravagant clothing at the most inappropriate times. She constantly needs to be flattered and admired, and she measures her success in terms of material objects.

Stepford wives think nothing of plunking down $50,000 in one store on any given afternoon. They are shopping cyclones. Between shopping sprees, consulting with interior designers, attending or organizing luncheons, semiannual visits to the plastic surgeon, and expensive health spas, their calendars are jam-packed. Speaking a fashion language so professional one would think they were in the business, they cultivate fashion to the point where their wardrobe is their occupation, fashion shows and charity benefits their stomping grounds.

PERSONAL CHANGE GOALS FOR THE STEPFORD WIFE

Many of the goals set for the extremist (and for the perfectionist and conformist, about whom we'll talk shortly) are also useful for the Stepford wife.

If you see yourself as a Stepford wife, realize that although you spend a great deal of time and attention on your appearance, the world is made of people with vastly different appearances. Look outside yourself and see how the rest of the world looks. Examine the various ways people present themselves and how they interact with one another. Often their clothing plays only a small role in their interactions. If you have trouble downscaling your approach to appearance, try using imagery. Imagine getting dressed without an elaborate plan or without applying makeup. Use positive thoughts and affirmations to make this image more comfortable.

For years, women have been encouraged to derive their self-esteem from their husbands. This approach is ineffective and is losing its clout as a societal norm. Recognize that your husband and children are very important in your life but are not a seamless extension of yourself. Work on your own vision of the world and of your role in that world. Set goals for personal growth and plan strategies to achieve them. Discover a potential career interest or put your energy toward a cause you believe in (political, social, environmental). Improve your relationships with others by trying to see them as they really are, rather than trying to see your reflection in them. As you work to claim your vision, the material temptations become less seductive.

WARDROBE GOALS FOR
THE STEPFORD WIFE

The next time you feel the gnawing desire to go out and buy extravagant clothing, stop and ask yourself what you are trying to achieve. Be creative—try to make something you already have look new and different. *Keep your look "approachable."* Your appearance should reflect the real you. Keep in mind that the validation you seek in trying to be the most impressively dressed woman in the room is illusionary. So much more is earned by walking into a room and sensing the warmth from others who respect your wit, kindness, or intelligence.

HOW TO SPOT A STEPFORD WIFE

♦ Lynx and sable furs

♦ Jockey caps and riding clothes for weekends (brand new, of course)

♦ Fox stoles thrown over slinky gowns

♦ Jeweled, custom-made lipstick cases

♦ Shih tzus or poodles with names like Kierkegaard or Hamlet

♦ Bottega Veneta evening bags

♦ Rolex or Patek Philippe watches

- Keiselstein-Cord jewelry and belts

- Cartier coin earrings and necklace

- Cheek implants

- Crocodile Hermès Kelly bag

- Lots of red and other brightly colored clothing

- Little girl couture (party gowns with lots of ruffles)

- Pouf dresses

- Silk parkas with reversible mink lining

- Manolo Blahnik jewel-encrusted mules

- Huge estate jewels (preferably Fred Leighton, Frances Klein)

- Personal secretary to organize dinners and charity affairs

- Silent ownership of a small boutique in a tony neighborhood

- Personal, custom-made perfume scents

- Pearl-and-diamond chokers, preferably from the 1930s or 1940s

- Baby-doll dresses with gazar sashes in bright colors

- Perfectly manicured red nails

- Baume & Mercier diamonds

- Unmovable hairdos

- Breathy voices

- Louis Vuitton luggage

- Poised smile, ever ready for the camera

- Blond and red one-tone hair with streaks running from ash blond to gold

- Taut faces

- Perfect makeup

- Elaborate silk cover-ups for the pool or beach

- Western wear, preferably Ralph Lauren for boom town hoedown parties

THE CONFORMIST

"The greatest mistake you can make in life is to be continually fearing you will make one."
                                                        —*E. Hubbard*

To find the conformist in a crowd, look for the woman who doesn't stand out. The conformist feels most comfortable when belonging to a group. She is overly concerned with what other people will say. The approval of others is more important than her own opinions, and she gauges her own style by what those she respects are wearing, often calling these "fashion cheerleaders" to find out what they'll be wearing to an event. She dresses for her women friends, often obviously mimicking them. Once the conformist finds the "approved" style, she sticks with it, going to the same beauty salon as her friends and adhering to one "acceptable" designer.

Deeply fearful of looking "different," the conformist is extremely sensitive to criticism and terrified of being ridiculed or not accepted. As a result, decision making is painful. An underdeveloped sense of her own identity means that the opinions and approval of others are crucial. Such women are obsessed with being on the right committee, going to the right schools and parties, and having the right clothes and right interior decor for their homes.

While most people consider the prospect of wearing a uniform limiting, conformists actually prefer it—as long as it is of the couture variety. Their clothing is their passport into a society in which women are judged according to particular codes of behavior and dress. Not only is it a comfort to be with others like themselves, but conformists also avoid the potentially threatening task of making any stylistic or aesthetic decisions. They're usually afraid to take a chance by wearing something extraordinary, even if it may actually look great on them.

This type of "homogenized dressing" was apparent at a recent show held to raise money for cancer research. The scene was divided into four camps. On one side sat a group of leopard-spandexed starlets in Barbarella headbands with dangerously high pumps dangling from their StairMaster-toned legs. Across the room sat an inanimate group of paper doll–like women from the lunch circuit in Chanel or Escada suits, beauty parlor hair, and too much jewelry. In another corner, a group of serious women was dressed in variations of Armani gear, their eyes shielded by Armani sunglasses, their feet clad in heavy-soled oxfords. Yet another grouping consisted of women paying homage to the designer of the month. But among all of these women, not *one* actually possessed her own style.

Conformists are armed with a sneer of cynicism for anyone whose appearance differs from theirs, and it stems from their own fear of being shunned and ridiculed for not fitting in. Wearing the same "uniform" as their peers masks the conformist's fear of rejection. She avoids any style that might stir up controversy; and since she cannot trust her own judgment, she feels safest choosing one formula and sticking to it.

Personal Change Goals for the Conformist

The conformist's suppressed sense of identity makes outside opinions crucial. She discounts her own taste and decision-making abilities. Try to remember where you first got the message that being "different" was "bad." Fill in the blank: "I don't trust my judgment/opinion/self because ___." Are your responses founded in reality? Do you actually have bad taste, or was your style criticized for some other reason? Do you really make poor decisions, or was your sense of competence undermined at some point in the past? Discover the parts of yourself that have been silenced, and begin to speak for yourself again. Next, ask yourself what validation by your peers provides. Recognize that the approval of others is no substitute for self-acceptance. You are unique; learn to acknowledge and celebrate that.

WARDROBE GOALS FOR THE CONFORMIST

Express your sense of self by deviating from your standard style. Take small steps at first; change comes gradually. You might begin by wearing *your* favorite type of underwear!

If slinky is in but you love cotton, wear cotton—no one but you will know. Use splashes of your favorite colors in scarves, socks, or hair accessories, even if they're not the colors the trend predictors have decreed are "in." As you come to realize that others still care for you regardless of your style, you'll gain confidence and be able to bend the rules to suit your own taste. Let the goal be to make your clothing choices according to the occasion and your frame of mind. Trust your judgment, remembering that it's the *person* who makes the clothes—not the other way around.

HOW TO SPOT A CONFORMIST

- ◆ Cowboy boots

- ◆ Ralph Lauren clothes with visible emblem

- ◆ Morganthal Fredericks eyeglasses

- ◆ Cartier watches

- Baseball caps

- Keiselstein-Cord belts

- Perfect red fingernails

- French manicures

- Armani suits

- Bottega Veneta handbags

- Beauty parlor shoulder-length or chin-length bobs with bangs

- Ferragamo pumps

- Louis Vuitton makeup trunk

- Chanel quilted bag

- Belgian loafers

- Adolpho suits

- Hermès blouson jackets

- Celine bags

- Oliver Peoples sunglasses

- ◆ Chanel suits

- ◆ Ballet slippers

- ◆ Tiffany's diamond *x* earrings

- ◆ Warm-up suits, preferably in silk

- ◆ Prada knapsack or quilted bag

- ◆ Pearl earrings and diamonds from Tiffany

- ◆ Mules

- ◆ Bardot chignons and topknots

THE PERFECTIONIST

The perfectionist never has a sloppy day. She is gripped by compulsive fastidiousness. If she thinks her appearance is flawed in any way, she feels uncomfortable and incomplete. Her need to fit a specific image fuels her look—and her life. She spends hours in pursuit of the best hairstyle, the perfect manicure, and the optimal workout to achieve the best figure—even the ideal surgically acquired features. The perfectionist panics if her looks don't meet her expectations and will even cancel appointments when she is not satisfied with her appearance. Overly judgmental and critical of herself, she bolsters her self-esteem and distances herself from others by intimidating them with her outward perfection. After all, who could get close to someone with such a perfect image? No matter how neat and put together another might be, when they're in the company of a perfectionist, they suddenly feel deficient, frumpy.

Whether it's hot, cold, or windy, the perfectionist always looks perfect—neatly coiffed with not a hair out of place, freshly polished nails, perfectly laundered and pressed garments. The problem with this type of fashion slave is that her image is too perfect to be real. She gives the impression that she wakes up looking impeccable, when the truth is she spends so many hours attending to her appearance, she hardly has time for anything else.

Typically, someone overly meticulous about her looks has some type of conflict in her life that she's not dealing with. The sense of control she feels in managing her appearance so fastidiously is probably an attempt to compensate for the lack of control she feels in other, more significant areas of her life. Unfortunately, the time and energy devoted to such compulsive activity prevents her from examining the root cause of her need for control.

Most of us are concerned about our appearance and get a great feeling knowing we look attractive, stylish, and well groomed. But if we can't relax or feel all right about ourselves unless our appearance is absolutely perfect, that healthy concern becomes an unhealthy obsession.

PERSONAL CHANGE GOALS
FOR THE PERFECTIONIST

Recognize that the need to present a perfect appearance may be a way to avoid facing disturbing issues in your life. Start to identify and face your anxieties; talk about them with a friend or counselor, and try to shift focus from your outer self to what's going on inside you.

Begin to relax your compulsive defenses. Learn to accept your imperfections (an undeniable aspect of the human condition), and extend that acceptance to others as well. Keep in mind that in the struggle to control and contain your appearance, you are really *being controlled* by your own anxieties.

WARDROBE GOALS FOR THE PERFECTIONIST

Experiment with a "let it all hang out" day (or hour). Try to let one or two things in your appearance go in situations where no one will notice. For example, skip the makeup during your workout or wear old sweats while you read the paper on Sunday mornings.

When you get comfortable with that, allow yourself similar slack in situations with one or two friends or in semipublic circumstances.

Wear sneakers and carry your heels. Invite a friend for lunch at home, and dress in a more relaxed way than you're used to. You'll be pleasantly surprised to learn that people *will* care about you— even without your mascara and hair gel. Turn your "imperfections" into your unique beauty asset. Keep in mind Brooke Shields's eyebrows, the space between Lauren Hutton's front teeth, and Cindy Crawford's mole!

How to Spot a Perfectionist

◆ Real jewelry (fake is too gauche)

◆ Cashmere capes or sweater sets

◆ Custom-made hats

◆ Standing manicure and hair appointments twice a week

◆ Matching accessories

◆ Coordinated outfits

◆ Buttoned-up suits and shirts

◆ Stiffly constricted handbag in hard leather

◆ Perfectly coiffed hair

◆ Defined makeup

◆ Duplicate outfits and gowns

◆ One style of shoes in many colors

◆ Electronic or cataloged closets with pictures of every outfit completely accessorized

STATUS SIGNALS

*"People have declaimed against luxury for 2,000 years, in
verse and in prose, and people have always delighted in it."*
—*Voltaire*

"Mirror, mirror, on the wall, am I really chic after all?"

A handsome woman studies herself before a full-length mirror at
the Chanel boutique in Beverly Hills. A raspberry-, pink-, and
white-checked Chanel suit from the fall collection frames her body.
Gold chains and pearls cascade down the front of her jacket. The
image reflected back to her is fashionable, self-assured, powerful.

The salesgirl nods in approval. "You look stunning," she
exclaims.

"I'll take it," replies the customer.

The lure of status symbols is extremely seductive, and few are
able to resist succumbing entirely. We invest in a Chanel suit not
only because it flatters us and makes us feel like the million bucks
it probably cost, but because in so doing, we align ourselves with a
label that's synonymous with quality and design. It provides us an
unassailable sense of fashion security.

On another level, status wear functions as a way of defining ourselves as members of a particular social stratum or constituency. A
Rolex or Patek Philippe watch, a Hermès bag, or Bulgari jewelry
flash a distinct and instantaneous message of economic and social
privilege.

When we meet someone wearing these same status accessories,
we assume she shares our values and beliefs and feel more comfortable in her presence. Indeed, we are all searching for kindred spirits and are more likely to find one in the person who sports a style
comparable to ours than the one whose clothes speak a foreign
language.

DRESS CODE

Status symbol garments and the distinctive "uniforms" of certain designers associated with luxury and social status connote a glamorous and privileged lifestyle, and that association is what many women are buying when they purchase these clothes. Beyond the automatic status designer fashions confer on the wearer, there is the vicarious escape into a way of life that we perceive to be more exciting, refined, or exotic than our own. And who among us would not gladly welcome the romantic aspects of a privileged, aristocratic life if we had the choice?

In the past, aristocratic women were obliged to wear garments that laced and buttoned them in as firmly as possible, because constricting clothes that made manual labor impossible were a sign of wealth. Crinolines, trains, and tightly fastened corsets that seriously hampered a woman's physical movements proclaimed that these privileged souls had servants to do such work for them. Hobble skirts in extravagant fabrics signified that the wearer would never be required to engage in an activity that might soil her fine clothes.

Today, women of high economic standing need not be constrained to appear privileged; even the most exclusive designers offer fashions to fit a variety of lifestyles. And those who merely aspire to such lifestyles can wear the fashions and live vicariously. Consumers of costly designer wear can transport themselves to any of a vast array of environments, time zones, or moods.

CONSPICUOUS VERSUS SUBTLE STATUS

"When a woman chooses to wear Chanel or Valentino, she actually has already made up her mind and has decided to look rich and to belong to a socially high class."

—Gianni Versace

Have you ever noticed how the preeminent pieces in a name designer's collection are usually those that most obviously bear his or her stamp? Were you also aware that often the most creative and beautifully designed items do not reveal the designer's identity and therefore don't sell as well?

This is because, for many women, the primary reason for wearing designer clothes is so others will *know* that they're wearing designer clothes. The woman whose highest priority is flashing the designer identity of her clothing will wear an exquisite designer scarf so that the designer's name is more obvious than the design. On the other hand, the person who's more concerned with showing off the aesthetic attributes of her scarf will select one on that basis. This is the essential distinction between subtle and conspicuous status.

CONSPICUOUS STATUS

The woman who enjoys the adornment of conspicuous status symbols tends to be more approval oriented. She spends a lot of money on readily recognized designer clothing and luxury items, pieces that shout their worth to others. For such a woman, it is important that people are clearly aware of the statement she makes through her clothing, and she blatantly embellishes herself with outward labels—a Chanel suit, Louis Vuitton bags, or Keiselstein-Cord accessories, for example.

The fashion extrovert enjoys the challenge of keeping pace with the latest fashion looks touted by the media and is very trend sensitive. Her purchases tell others that she can afford to keep up with the whims of fashion.

Conspicuous labels also offer a reassuring sense of fashion security. Many women derive confidence from wearing something that clearly states to the world, "If you don't think this is tasteful, you're wrong, because everyone knows that Gucci [or Louis Vuitton, or Chanel] is in good taste." If something is obviously expensive, in theory it *must* be of superior quality.

Such a culture-driven psychodynamic frees a woman from worrying about her own choices and putting her unique stamp or statement on the styles she wears. Rather than having to determine just what such a statement might be, all she has to do is bear the right trademark.

Unfortunately, this modus operandi may send the following unintended messages:

- ◆ "I must wear my designer labels on my sleeve because I need the approval of others and feel this is the only way to get it."

♦ "I'm compelled to wear obvious status styles because I fear making more individualistic fashion choices."

♦ "Status symbols are very important, and if you don't share this belief, I'm not interested in knowing you."

COMMONSENSE GUIDELINES FOR THE CONSPICUOUS STATUS WEARER

Even if you're a conspicuous status wearer, it's important to select only those styles that are suitable for *you,* ensuring that your wardrobe reflects your individual taste and aesthetic. Avoid jumping on the bandwagon of every passing trend. Instead discriminate in favor of those designer offerings that show you off in the best possible light.

CONSPICUOUS STATUS SYMBOLS

◆ Jockey caps and riding clothes for weekends (brand new)

◆ Keiselstein-Cord jewelry and belts

◆ Cartier coin earrings and necklace

◆ Velvet or suede shoes with visible emblems

◆ Manolo Blahnik jewel-encrusted mules

◆ Huge estate jewels (preferably Fred Leighton, Frances Klein)

◆ Pearl-and-diamond chokers (preferably from the 1930s or 1940s)

◆ Baby-doll dresses with gazar sashes in bright colors

◆ Perfectly manicured red nails

◆ Cowboy boots in pristine condition

◆ Ralph Lauren clothes with visible emblem

◆ Cartier watches and rolling rings

◆ Baseball caps

- Black leather beeper cases and cellular phone cases disguised as evening bags

- Gold sequin, metallic, or jeweled baseball caps

- Leather jeans

- Baseball jackets made out of designer scarfs

- Belgian loafers

- Harry & Son jodhpurs

- Cowboy and cowgirl chic clothes; suede skirts with fringes

- Louis Vuitton makeup trunk

- Chanel quilted bag

- Adolpho suits

- Hermès blouson jackets

- Oliver Peoples sunglasses

- Louis Vuitton luggage

- Evening bags from Judith Leiber

SUBTLE STATUS

The woman of subtle status keeps her labels tucked inside her clothes, preferring to let the fabric and cut of her garments speak for themselves. She is the type who studiously avoids displaying initials and insignias. If her status outfit is recognized at all, it will be by those whose understanding and aesthetic are similar to hers. She is elegant yet subdued, and whether she seeks out classic or individualistic styles, her main objective is to look tasteful and please herself.

Every season, the woman of subtle status buys a few suits, favoring the refined tailoring and luxurious fabrics of Armani, Prada, or Zoran. You'll find her nursing a cappuccino at an outdoor cafe, swathed in a cream-colored cashmere sweater, flannel trousers, and Hermès scarf.

For evening she might wear an unadorned sheath from Calvin Klein or a tuxedo smoking jacket from Donna Karan or Yves Saint Laurent. She looks for fabrics that feel sensuous against her skin but are somewhat conservative. Once she finds a style that suits her, she sticks with it, rather than acquiescing to every runway whim. She buys clothes that remain fashionable and wear for years.

Her accessories are subtle as well. One will glimpse only a wedding band and perhaps a striking antique pin affixed to the lapel of her jacket or a sensuous pair of Ted Muehling earrings.

Casual wear in extravagant fabrics is another discreet expression of status that appeals to those who don't feel compelled to flaunt their wealth or good taste. Short trench coats in candy-colored shades of organza, silk or satin anoraks, velvet or cashmere jogging suits, and cashmere peacoats are all examples of subtle status. When we buy elegant casual wear we communicate that we have the income to treat valuable possessions nonchalantly, without worrying about ruining or dirtying them.

140

Capturing the spirit of an earlier aristocratic era is also an element of subtle or "silent status." The look Grace Kelly popularized in the 1950s—cashmere sweater sets, sleeveless silk tanks, linen suits, the ubiquitous Hermès scarf tied around her head and neck, and the battered Kelly bag—harkens back to a more genteel time. Variations on this look are still popular in Palm Beach and elite hangouts in Europe.

When we adapt the image of subtle status, we project a sense of elegant simplicity and upper-class charm. We convey that we value nice things but don't wear them in order to elicit respect or envy. Our style reflects our preference for quality and good taste while at the same time signifying a relaxed attitude about our appearance.

SIGNALS OF SUBTLE STATUS

◆ Prada silk clothing

◆ Harriet Selwyn clothing

◆ Jil Sander suits

◆ Robert Clergerie shoes

◆ Missoni separates

◆ Ted Muehling jewelry

◆ Robert Lee Morris jewelry and belts

◆ Cashmere capes and sweater sets

◆ Custom-made hats

◆ Cashmere leggings (especially by Fogal)

◆ Anything by Zoran

◆ Crocodile shoes

◆ Calvin Klein suits

◆ Hermès jodhpurs

◆ Patek Philippe watches

◆ Harry Winston jewelry

◆ Calvin Klein or Perry Ellis cashmere overcoats

◆ Silk parkas with reversible mink lining

◆ Hermès leather notepads

IS IT OKAY TO BE STATUS CONSCIOUS?

Regardless of our income level or how highly we prize being fashionable, each of us is in some way vulnerable to the allure of fashion status symbols. It's really nothing to be ashamed of. For the most part, haute couture designers deserve the acclaim they receive and the fanfare that surrounds them. They're creative people who excel in their field, and it makes sense that those who can afford to do so would want to purchase their designs.

But our desire or need for such goods must be placed in the proper perspective.

Good taste—even a taste for luxury and elegance—doesn't require that you either confine your purchases to recognizable "name clothing" or spend a fortune.

Actually, it has as much to do with *avoiding* unflattering trends as keeping up with the styles that allow you to shine. Good taste means being aware of your own fashion persona and creatively combining those various stylistic components that most attractively reflect your personal look.

No matter how much you admire a certain status designer, *you* are ultimately the best "designer" and manager of your own wardrobe, because only you know which fashions most truly express the authentic you.

HOW TO MAKE DESIGNER FASHIONS WORK FOR YOU

Given that most of us are not about to spend half a year's salary on a dress we'd be too embarrassed or frightened to wear, to what extent can we enjoy—within our means—the best that designer wear has to offer without becoming "label slaves"? The designer rule of thumb: Consider good taste and appropriateness first, labels second. Regardless of how highly touted a particular designer is, if his or her fashions don't happen to look good on *you*, they have no place in your closet.

After honestly thinking about your fashion persona, do your homework and find out which designers you have the most in common with. Read current fashion magazines and try to discover the "attitudes" various designers attempt to capture in their designs; see if you can relate to either their philosophy or their fashions. "Window-shop" (don't buy anything yet) to get an idea of what such fashions look and feel like "in person."

Next, examine your closet to determine how the new "must have" outfit works with what you already have. Consider the practicality and longevity of what you plan to buy. Will it likely be a staple in your wardrobe, or will you have little use for it, given your lifestyle? Can you see yourself wearing it for years to come, or is it a fleeting fad that will be outdated in less than a year? Most important, is it *really* you, or are you being swayed by status symbol hype?

Designer fashions that are inappropriate for your individual look and lifestyle make you appear "out of sync" with yourself and *send one or more of the following negative messages:*

- ◆ "I don't trust my own instincts. I dress like this to avoid the threatening task of making any stylistic or aesthetic decision on my own."

- ◆ "I measure my success in terms of material items, which is why I had to have this dress that looks wrong on me."

- ◆ "I so need to be accepted by others and to fit in by wearing the 'in' designer clothing that I am unaware of how foolish I look in this outfit."

Tasteful, appropriate designer styles send these messages:

- ◆ "The way I look reflects something authentic about me."

- ◆ "I dress this way because I honestly feel it is a becoming, suitable style for me."

♦ "I feel relaxed in this outfit."

EVERY LABEL TELLS A STORY

As you begin to think about how to integrate designer styles into your wardrobe, consider not only the current fashions you find on display in fashionable boutiques and high-end department stores but the reputation each has earned over the years. Each designer has a consistent image that pervades his or her collection. The following will help you chart your course through the haute couture network.

Gianni Versace caters to rock-and-roll personalities, trendsetters, and some of Hollywood's elite with his bold, racy, electric, clothing. His styles project a sexy image of flash and fantasy.

Valentino usually appeals to the sophisticated woman who moves easily and frequently in international society.

Geoffrey Beene is popular with a refined, intelligent, cosmopolitan clientele.

The Armani image embodies a kind of reverse snobbism, suggestive of a woman who has lifted herself above the dictates of fashion. With its hip cult following, Armani styles have become closely associated with the entertainment industry. Women shell out a great deal of money for Armani yet still look understated, safe.

Donna Karan's appeal is unabashedly to women in positions of power. The look is that of an accomplished, busy individual who has earned her success. She might be at the top of the corporate ladder, perhaps president of her own company, a high government official, or a television personality.

Such a high-powered professional image is a stark contrast to

Assedine Alaia's flirtatious sexpot look. Worn by models and entertainers with hard-edged bodies, these clinging, body-sculpting outfits exude youthful sexuality.

Ralph Lauren is more than a designer label; it is reflective of an entire lifestyle. The woman who wears Ralph Lauren clothing seeks a world where unharried people on ponies play polo in freshly mowed fields. Lauren's western wear and Aztec look re-create the gentility and refinement of previous generations. He lures us into a number of different gracious, luxurious environments: the adventurous world of safari, the good life in America, the spiritual life of the Aztec Indians. Women feel they, too, can enjoy some aspect of these lifestyles by slipping into a Ralph Lauren garment.

Followers of Bill Blass, Oscar de la Renta, and Arnold Scassi often live lives as privileged as the designers they patronize.

Dior (Gianfranco Ferre), Yves Saint Laurent, and Givenchy also cater to a select group of jet-setters who not only wear their clothes but frequently socialize with them as well. These customers may even engage their designers in advice on interior design and other aesthetic aspects of their lives.

In contrast with the more reserved finery and genteel images of the great couturiers, Jean Paul Gaultier and Thierry Mugler have positioned themselves in the glitterati avant, catering to an eclectic mix of rock stars, actresses, and denizens of the underworld.

BREAKING THE CHAINS OF FASHION SLAVERY

The unrelenting quest to be fashionable is usually undertaken to fill not a closet but rather a personal void. Of course the only way this emptiness can be filled is by valuing yourself and gaining satisfaction through your interests, endeavors, and relationships. When you learn to appreciate your uniqueness and enjoy who you are, you'll no longer struggle to "keep up" with the latest fashion trends. Instead, a style uniquely your own will emerge.

A woman's fashion compass should come from within. When you're aware of what works for you, you'll take pride in that aesthetic and, within the boundaries of good taste, project the person you truly are.

Role-Playing: Reinventing Yourself with Fashion

"A man never reveals his character more vividly than when portraying the character of another."
— *Jean Paul Richter*

Although designer labels and status clothing convey a sense of wealth and power, our fashion choices are often motivated by something beyond the wish simply to appear tasteful and elegant. Within each of us is a certain desire for fantasy, an inclination to experience something dramatically different from our everyday reality—at least vicariously. Slipping into a particular outfit, we can "role-play" by projecting ourselves into lifestyles and environments bearing little resemblance to our own.

As long as it is approached in such a way as to emphasize the individuality of the wearer, fashion role-playing can be a positive adventure. In this chapter we'll explore a number of different appealing "roles" and offer guidelines for "playing" each look to your unique advantage.

Getting dressed doesn't always have to be a serious affair. We spend so much time worrying about making the proper impression at work or when fulfilling social obligations; we're entitled to have some fun with fashion on occasion!

Role-playing can take us back to the days when, as little girls, we could dress up and feel the magic of slipping instantly into a new identity. Remember, as Halloween approached, how your friends would inquire excitedly, "What are you going to be this year?" Isn't there some part of that thrilling experience that still appeals to you?

I'm not implying that the kinds of fashions described in this chapter are costumes or that the effect on those who encounter you in "the ballerina look" or "equestrian chic" will be similar to that of encountering a child dressed up on Halloween. The object is to tailor such role-playing styles to your own personal aesthetic so that the effect is more integrated than jarring.

"Fantasy and romance play a huge role in fashion. I have seen women buy clothes and say 'this will be wonderful to wear to Ascot' even though the chances of their going to Ascot that season are very very slim. It has to do with fantasy."
—*Bill Blass*

Regardless of the particular genre you find most appealing, fashion role-playing can breathe new life into a humdrum wardrobe, express aspects of your personality you don't otherwise get a chance to expose, even inspire you to make more meaningful changes in your life. On the other hand, sometimes women just want to have fun!

THE YOUTH ILLUSION

Teenagers—those fascinating and exasperating creatures—are caught between childhood and the adult world. While hormones rage, their tumultuous emotions are often expressed through their clothing choices. One minute a teenage girl is a vamp in tight jeans and a midriff top, the next she's shrouded in the androgynous look. The swing of her style pendulum reflects a struggle between her desire to express an emerging sexuality and her fear of it.

"I hate when I see a young woman who dresses like an older woman and an older woman who dresses as a very young woman. Where one finishes the other starts."—Valentino

---

When a grown women dons teenage fashions, it is important to understand the message that comes through; often she is also experiencing and expressing some conflict. Presenting oneself as young and sexual, showing off your body and trying to attract sexual attention, may be an unconscious attempt to deny the process of aging. A sixteen-year old girl is expected to emulate the latest MTV superstar, but when a middle-aged woman adopts the same look, she may seem to convey that she's not ready to accept the responsibility of being a mature adult, strive for adult goals, become emotionally grounded, or maintain adult relationships.

Adolescent clothing appeals to women for other reasons as well. A teenager can look like a prairie princess one day and a home girl the next. Since young people are engaged in a personal search for identity, their styles change regularly; they don't have to commit to any one in particular. But while the choices seem endless when we're young, as we grow older they appear more limited. Youth seems to hold more promise—more to look forward to and to risk. The attitudes that define the youthful experience are more tempting to some adults than mature values.

It makes sense in our youth-oriented culture that women forever wish to be at a stage of life other than the one they're at. Psychologists call this "developmental discontinuity." The twelve-year-old can't wait to wear the makeup and clothing of her sixteen-year-old sister—and be entitled to the same privileges as her older sibling. The teenager wants to be twenty-five. The thirty-five-year-old fears middle age and wants to look eighteen again. Perhaps because there is such a narrow definition of an attractive woman, all females try to look twenty years old, whether they are ten or sixty.

This phenomenon is partly media driven. The female ideal is the slim, vibrant twenty-year-old. Women are led to believe that no other age is as valuable. Such a perception has a "biological" basis in that the twenties are when women are most fertile and thus most desirable in terms of their reproductive power. Reproductive potential is an important factor in a man's judgment of a potential mate and in a woman's judgment of herself. With middle age comes the fear of being undesirable. Constant and fervent attempts to look younger relate directly to these basic fears. Dressing like a twenty-year-old is one way to cling to the traits that, at least partially, define femininity.

Waists are probably the most telltale indication of adolescence and young womanhood. Hip-hugging pants paired with a cropped top that reveal a narrow waist and flat tummy emphasize the time in a woman's life when those parts of her body have not yet widened from childbearing.

An older woman who diets to regain her slim youthfulness may yearn to recapture the look of a teenage girl, carefree and irresponsible, even though it is perfectly natural for her body to become rounder—and more voluptuous.

There are a number of teenage styles that some adult women find

appealing for various reasons. In choosing a particular teen fashion, you may be expressing your desire to return to some aspect of your childhood without even knowing it. As you read along, ask yourself how much space these youthful fashions are taking up in your closet.

Youthful styles appeal to mature women for many reasons, the most obvious being that they make us feel vital and up-to-date. But we need to be keenly aware of how others see us when we choose such fashions. A mature woman who adopts the clothing of a woman several decades younger can run the risk of looking inappropriate or just downright silly. This is not to say that once we pass thirty our skirts must fall safely to our knees or that a bare midriff is verboten to anyone over sixteen; it is simply a matter of balancing the sense of youthful energy these clothes confer on the wearer versus the way the outside world perceives them.

First, let's take a look at some of the reasons women are attracted to youthful fashions.

1. *Wearing clothes that were popular when we were young reconnects us to our youth.* Wanting to return to the clothing of our youth is a normal instinct. For some of us, re-creating a youthful appearance is payback for having been too busy hoisting ourselves up the career ladder or rearing children to have fully enjoyed our younger years. Perhaps you're attracted to particular styles you missed out on, such as the 1960s hippie look or the early 1980s new wave phase.

Then there are those who seek to reconnect with their youth by dressing in the fashions they wore when they felt the most popular or accomplished or when they were the happiest—whether it was high school or college days, debutante balls, or their commitment-free early twenties.

The woman who wears a bouffant hairdo or pageboy flip from twenty years ago may be clinging to a time when she was in the spotlight; the forty-five-year-old who feels that the 1960s were the most exciting years of her life may still sport waist-length hair, a slash of bright blue eye shadow, and ankle-length, floral-print dresses. But while she may feel buoyed by this connection with the past, others will see it differently. Her attire suggests that she is unable to leave that period of her life behind and insecure about acknowledging the number of years that have gone by since.

It seems so simple—choose a bygone period and relive it. Unfortunately, an older woman wearing the styles of her youth often communicates to others that she's either trying to masquerade as younger or is "stuck" in an era that has long since ended. The trick is to incorporate only those elements of beloved bygone-era fashions that are becoming on an adult woman of the nineties.

2. *Youthful fashions reflect a more carefree attitude.* Dressing young makes the statement that you're still not buying into the overly restrictive conventions that are attendant upon adulthood. We all yearn to be emancipated from the complexities of the adult world at times, but while a certain degree of fashion free-spiritedness is positive, dressing like a rebellious teenager can be detrimental to your social and professional lives both. Co-workers don't take a woman seriously when she shows up wearing ribbon-bound pigtails or grunge-inspired teen outfits. Dressing like an impish little girl or an angry adolescent instead of a grown woman suggests that you are not comfortable with your own maturity.

Attitudes concerning appropriate dress for forty-year-old and older women are being shaped, in part, by the baby boomers. Having been steeped in the culture of the 1960s when they were teenagers, they continue to espouse values that reflect a belief in spontaneity, freedom, and rebelliousness. Why shouldn't a forty-three-year-old woman wear a wild outfit if she wants to? What's wrong with playful experimentation in our clothing choices? "Who says I'm too old to still look 'hip'?" asks the middle-aged fashion consumer of the 1990s.

It's a fine line to walk, because each of us has a rebellious child inside us that wants out every now and then. What we need to be mindful of is the degree to which we let that child express herself.

3. *If my body is in great shape, why shouldn't I wear young-looking fashions that make the most of it?* The health and exercise movement is another reason women in their third and fourth decades and beyond look younger and feel entitled to wear fashions that show off their bodies. This is fine up to a point, but all you have to do is study a forty-five-year-old dressed in an ultrarevealing, gimmicky adolescent getup to conclude that she'd look

much more attractive in something more befitting a woman of her age. Again, as much as we may feel inclined to rebel against such a conservative concept, *moderation is the key* to youthful—yet taste-ful—role-playing.

THE BALLERINA LOOK

If you're drawn to

- short skirts in billowing tulle or pleated gabardine with hip- or waist-length jacket and satin lace-up or ankle-strapped pumps

- strapless tafetta-bodiced dresses with flared skirts and flat, satin lace-up shoes

- Lycra leggings and leotards in cotton-candy pinks and pale blues, with short, twirly skirts and leather ballet slippers

you're a ballerina at heart

From the time we were little girls, many of us have idealized the vision of the ethereal ballerina with her lithe body, cloudlike tutu, and dainty satin slippers. The ballerina is an icon of femininity, youth, beauty, and romance and at the same time represents hard work and discipline.

Many women continue to consider themselves "dancers at heart" long after they've hung up their toe shoes. *Women's Wear Daily* dubbed the woman who habitually dresses in leotards and Capezio slippers as the "city ballerina." Such a woman is likely to devote considerable time and effort to maintaining her body, keeping it

toned and flexible. Layered ballet attire—unitards in basic colors, topped by sweaters or soft, wrapped skirts and leggings, accented by bright accessories—make up a good part of her everyday wardrobe. She may carry an overstuffed tote bag rather than a purse and pull her hair back into a severe ponytail or chignon.

Designers have also adapted the ballet look in their collections, using many appealing variations: tight satin bodices with layers of tulle cascading from a nipped-in waistline; evening and street wear with tulle or crinoline skirts flaring out from jackets; and satin slippers that lace up the leg.

The dancer's uniform, in either its simplest or most stylized version, embues the wearer with an essential vitality and joie de vivre. The ballet look is a romantic, nonthreatening way to display the softer side of your femininity and athletic prowess. If you want to project the grace and ethereal quality of a Degas dancer, consider wearing the ballerina look to your next romantic encounter.

THE HODGEPODGE CHILD

If you're drawn to

- bright Crayola colors in exuberant combinations

- skirts or pants or shorts in one pattern paired with tops in another

- high-top colored tennis shoes with patterned ankle socks or socks in a contrasting color

you're just a kid who wants to have fun at heart.

Young children choose what appeals to them spontaneously, without regard for social approval. As they get older, the need to conform and win the approval of their peers will eventually govern their clothing choices. But before she reaches this stage, a child's joy is often expressed unconsciously through her clothing.

The bright colors children are naturally attracted to represent energy, enthusiasm, and excitement. When a little girl gets dressed in the morning she doesn't think in terms of "coordinating" her outfit; rather, she chooses each piece of clothing based on its own distinct attributes. A five-year-old's typical outfit can combine a pair of pink tights, a yellow skirt, and a red T-shirt, all topped off with flowered socks, patterned tennis shoes, and a Barney lunch box.

Interestingly, some women return to a modified version of this look as adults. The excessive decoration and hodgepodge of colors have a primitive feel, and a woman who favors this look seems to be in touch with her more primal impulses, which can be a very endearing trait. On the flip side, however, a whimsical, childish look encourages others to think of you as whimsical and childlike and is therefore not appropriate for business situations or any time you want to convey authority and strong presence. Save your multicolored patchwork of styles to enliven Saturday's volleyball game or casual picnic with close friends—who know you well enough to accept your inner kid.

THE BABY-DOLL LOOK

If these are your idea of heaven

◆ voluminous crinoline and taffeta circle skirts, embellished with darling flowers, wide gazar sashes, and adorable dangling ribbons

◆ little girl pinafores and frocks

◆ Cinderella ball gowns with wide satin bows pinned to the derriere

◆ polka-dotted hair ribbons

◆ feminine, little girl sailor suits

◆ patent-leather "Mary Janes" with white ruffled ankle socks

then you're going for baby-doll style.

The "baby doll" look has returned to the fashion pages with a vengeance. Strapless taffeta dresses with circle skirts in extravagant, ornate fabrics and poufs in candy-colored cotton pastels are quite the rage for grown women.

DRESS CODE

High-waisted baby-doll jumpers and dresses worn with tiny, hand-held pocketbooks create an image strikingly reminiscent of little girls dressing up in their mother's clothes, their bodies hidden under folds of rich, cloudlike fabrics. Wearing such fashions as an adult, we recall our own small feet stumbling around in Mom's high heels, delighting at the "grown-up" vision we saw in Mommy's full-length mirror.

Dressing like a baby doll also provides a refreshing counterpoint to the harried pace and increased responsibilities women have assumed over the past several decades. What better way to forget a harrowing day at the office than to slip into a polka-dotted flounce skirt in resplendent layers of chiffon and lace? Not for every woman, but a fantasy come true for some.

Baby-Doll Element	Why It's Appealing
◆ bows	symbol of little girl innocence
◆ flounced skirts	reminiscent of dress-up birthday parties
◆ crushed-velvet tights	elegant yet innocently opaque
◆ embroidered dresses with tiny pearls and lace	have an aura of sweetness

Baby-doll fashions appeal to many women because they make them feel sweet, demure, or exuberant. Others claim wearing baby-doll clothes is a way to indulge their "take me under your wing" fantasies. Another faction reports that it's their boyfriends or husbands who encourage them to dress this way, because they find such a look both romantic and sexy. When we slip into this particular fashion fantasy, we revert to a time in life when everything is safe and delightful—when, shielded from life's turmoil and complexities, we could playfully relish the act of dressing up for a party as much as the party itself.

When a woman wears baby-doll-inspired fashions—rendered in more somber fabrics such as wool gabardine or tartan plaid—to work, it could be an unconscious attempt to coyly influence her male co-workers or boss as she once did her father or other loving adults. Clearly, using such a ploy ultimately undermines a woman's ability to develop the skills she needs to make her way in the world.

Even if this is not your intention, dressing in this way could be read by your co-workers as an attempt to shirk adult responsibilities. For this reason it's best to confine your baby-doll role-playing to romantic or social occasions.

THE PRESCHOOL LOOK

If you often wear

- ◆ sweatshirts or T-shirts appliquéd with any lovable animal or cartoon character

- ◆ pastel T-shirts embellished with dainty lace, pearls, or ruffles

- ◆ soft flannel dresses with empire waist or childlike smocking

- overall shorts with button down with T-shirt, knee-high socks, and oxfords

- peacoat with short pleated skirt

- plaid knapsacks

you like to pamper the little girl in you.
Closely related to both the "hodgepodge" and "baby doll" looks, the "preschool look" appeals to our need to express vulnerability and playfulness and to our occasional desire to be babied.

Brightly colored sweatshirts and ruffled skirts are part of the would-be little girl wardrobe, as are garments with princess or sweetheart necklines. Short ruffled skirts worn with cowboy boots, jeans and brightly colored sweatshirts, shirts or sweaters decorated with cartoon characters—all signal a covert longing to return to the carefree pleasures of childhood playtime by echoing the mood of school playgrounds and day-care centers. Needless to say, this is not an appropriate style for the office or a meeting with your child's teacher, but it's fine for lounging around on a weekend or attending very informal social gatherings.

THE PREPUBESCENT SCHOOLGIRL

If you love to wear

- skirts with cotton lace peering out underneath

- crisp white blouses with Peter Pan collars

- wool jumpers

- plaid pleated skirts held up with suspenders

- leather loafers and ankle socks

you may still yearn for the first day of school.

The back-to-school look of girlish innocence is yet another image women find very appealing, as it signifies a demure earnestness. Mia Farrow reflected these qualities when she wore Mary Quant's schoolgirl fashions in *Rosemary's Baby.* It is not uncommon to see a mother wearing a pleated miniskirt jumper, starched white blouse, and a floppy red bow tie while accompanying her daughter to school. Wearing clothing that is strongly reminiscent of her own school days allows her to live vicariously through her daughter and recapture a time of life she remembers fondly. The excitement of getting dressed for the first day of school and the fresh start a new school year signifies still linger in her mind and draw her to schoolgirl fashions.

This style may be appropriate in certain work environments if the outfit befits a more adult look—for example, knee-length jumpers worn with low heels and either long-sleeved turtleneck tops or Peter Pan–collared blouses.

THE TOMBOY LOOK

If you're drawn to

- boyish pants and shirts

- thick-soled shoes or sneakers

- striped T-shirts

- cardigan sweatshirts with zipper and hood

◆ baseball caps

you'd probably rather go climb a tree or throw a ball than go shopping.
Women who have fond memories of days spent climbing trees,
building forts, and being up at bat against the rest of the "guys" may
seek to re-create that period by dressing like an athletic little boy.
This is a comfortable style for recreational activities or casual social-
izing but when carried to an extreme may connote a sense of being
uncomfortable with one's femininity or sexuality.

THE PREP SCHOOL LOOK

If you wear

◆ polo shirts

◆ madras skirts, dresses, shirts, and pants

◆ pert, sorority girl hairstyles held in place with Pappagallo
headbands

◆ Pappagallo shoes

◆ Fair Isle sweaters

◆ tweed "boarding school blazers" by Brooks Brothers or
Ralph Lauren, navy blue blazers, or blazers with crests

◆ duck pants

◆ wire-rimmed glasses

- Top-Sider shoes

- well-laundered T-shirts from your prep school alma mater

- boxer shorts in odd, nondescript prints

- down vests

- tan raincoats

- floppy bow ties

you love to relive your prep school days.

Prep school attire is alive and well for many women whose prep school days are long gone; a trip to any suburban country club will confirm this. Such fashions make grown women feel comfortable because they hark back to a safe, youthful world.

The downside to this look is that it often gets overused. Some women feel so comfortable and "safe" in their madras skirts, neutral-colored polo shirts, and tan flats that they wear them like a uniform to every casual outing. Such outfits, when overworn in this way, tend to brand the wearer as bland and unimaginative. If you have a penchant for the preppie look, use it in moderation; on occasion try to experiment with other looks that tap into a different side of your personality.

THE SEXY TEEN LOOK

If you like

- ripped jeans or shorts slung low on the hips

- tight T-shirts that outline the breasts, tucked into tight jeans

DRESS CODE

- Lycra spandex print dresses worn with hoop earrings and charm bracelets

- flower print, body-skimming sundresses with flounced ruffled bottoms (the tightness of the dress and the flowering print symbolize the ambivalent struggle between sexuality and innocence)

you may be reliving the period of your own emerging sexuality.
This style may appeal to the woman who was overweight or forced to wear uniforms as a teenager and finally has the lifestyle and/or the figure to accommodate such sexy fashions. Fashions in this category emphasize budding sexuality and flash a message of sexual availability.

THE TOUGH TEEN LOOK

If your angry inner rebel likes to wear

- torn jeans

- leather jackets

- clunky black motorcycle boots with denim miniskirts

- multipierced ears and pierced noses

- wide leather belts with chunky buckles

you may be coming to terms with your "good girl" image.
This particular style allows grown women to experience in a safer, more controlled way the excitement, rebelliousness, and risk

taking they may have missed in their teenage years. The rough "rebel without a cause" look has enjoyed a passionate cult following ever since Marlon Brando and James Dean first rebelled in black leather forty years ago. Use your discretion in choosing this style; it's best for recreational and very casual situations.

BEYOND THE YOUTH ILLUSION

So where does a mature woman draw the line between youthful fun and age-appropriate dress? The challenge is to enjoy wearing the styles that appeal to you while at the same time not appearing foolish. Any of the previous youth looks are fine if they're not carried to an extreme or worn for anything other than very casual social or recreational occasions. These are fashions to have fun in, not to wear when conducting serious business.

It's also important to acknowledge the messages encoded in such styles. Be aware that when you wear your frilly baby-doll dress, you'll convey a certain sense of childish innocence—and helplessness; and that when you don the menacing black motorcycle jacket, onlookers will associate you with immature, rebellious tendencies. People who know you well will understand that you're a well-rounded, mature person who just happens to enjoy wearing such styles on occasion; strangers and those who know you casually may not draw the same conclusions.

RABBLE-ROUSER RAGS

Each season the fashion world wields its persuasive powers, admonishing women to keep up with the latest trends. Although there are myriad acceptable images from which to choose, many of us find the choices limiting and impractical. Others find it too time-consuming and expensive to keep up with fashion, and some feel that adhering to fashion codes inhibits their own style and personality.

Antifashion as a means of social defiance goes back to Marie Antoinette, the dandies, the bohemians of Lautrec's Paris, and the Malcolm Crowlyes in Greenwich Village. Each of these groups separated from society through the language of antifashion. Today, adopting an antifashion style is one way a woman can rebel against the rules of both the fashion industry and society at large.

It also allows her to choose styles that are more becoming on her particular figure and expressive of her individual aesthetic.

Those who wear antifashion clothing naturally represent nonconformity and originality. However, haute couture interpretations of antifashion do not convey the same meaning as the authentic garments. Their very reinterpretation distorts the original rebellious symbolism.

Today's revived hippie look, for example, carries none of the antifashion significance it once did; rather, it represents a very mainstream fashion statement. So the woman who wears a current designer's translation of a decades-past outrageous hippie style is in fact conforming, not rebelling. Designers may use an antifashion color, skirt length, or style, but the values and attitudes are clearly missing from their interpretations.

Through our authentic antifashion style we let others know we are unconventional in our thinking as well as in our look. People generally don't expect the woman in "rabble-rouser rags" to act like everyone else, and that's just the reaction those who wear such rags are after.

Following is an array of different rebellious styles. You might find one that expresses the real you, or perhaps you'll find yourself attracted to various articles of clothing from a number of different "genres."

BIKER/TOUGH GIRL CHIC

When you wear

♦ a heavy leather motorcycle jacket with lots of metal zippers

♦ black leather pants

♦ skintight jeans, T-shirt, and motorcycle boots

you reek of biker vibes.

Wearing biker clothing is a way to break out of the feminine mold and experience the sound and fury of the social renegade.

Since many women work at jobs that require conservative dress, biker chic provides an outlet for the pent-up frustrations of dealing with society's dictates. Looking slightly dangerous or threatening after hours is the perfect antidote to the safe, predictable image you're obliged to project from nine to five.

There is also a distinct element of romance attached to the biker culture. Roaring down the road on their powerful machines, alienated yet tough, bikers represent macho loners. When a woman laces up harness boots and puts on a studded leather jacket, she dons some very powerful symbols of freedom, strength, and rebellion.

A veritable mythology has arisen around the Hells Angels motorcycle group, and this legendary aura has spelled tremendous success for Harley-Davidson, which now puts their insignia on everything from T-shirts to swimsuits. In fact, they were recently given an award by the Council of Fashion Designers in recognition of their influence on the fashion industry!

ETHNIC ANTIFASHION

If you gravitate to exotic or ethnic looks such as

◆ Indian saris made from exquisite silks and cottons

◆ Mexican cotton peasant shirts and blouses and hand-embroidered "wedding dresses"

◆ shirts, dresses, and skirts made from richly colored, heavy Guatemalan cotton

◆ African dresses, hats, and dashikis

◆ Native American hair wraps, turquoise-and-silver jewelry

and belts, handmade leather moccasins

- padded silk "Mao jackets" from China

- Chinese silk "Nancy Kwan" dresses

- Balinese batik patchwork jackets with Chinese coin buttons

- hip-length silk Japanese kimonos, worn with wide silk pants

your style is multicultural.

Reaching out to another culture or aligning aesthetically with different ethnic groups is another form of antifashion. Retreating to a foreign culture for a sense of style is a kind of escape from mainstream society. The woman who chooses ethnic clothing communicates that she finds more beauty, vitality, and joy in the accoutrements of another culture than in the latest prestige couture.

She is making the social statement that the lifestyle and symbolism of the culture whose fashions she wears are preferable to what is available in modern Western society. Wearing the symbols of a more primitive culture is antifashion in that it denies the trappings of technoculture and reflects an appreciation of another culture's values and aesthetics. Traditional clothing from the Americas (like that of Native Americans from North and South America), India, the Middle East, Asia, and Africa—or fashions inspired by those cultures—offer myriad colorful and exotic styles, fabrics, and alternatives to Western dress.

A woman inspired by hip-hop, street fashions, and African culture might choose to wear dashikis or clothing made from African fabrics. If she is African American, her preference for these styles also sends a message of ethnic pride and social awareness and may bestow upon the wearer an increased sense of self-esteem.

Recording artist Queen Latifah launched the popularity of the African-inspired style, characterized by dashiki shirts in bright colors and crown hats woven of luminous "kente" cloth, a Ghanaian handwoven fabric. The outfit is topped off with kente bags, used originally for carrying healing herbs and other magic charms, and sashes made of kente cloth. African fashions also emphasize wrapped skirts, drummer pants, and other clothing in brilliant, vibrant tones. "Kufis," the crownlike hats, were originally worn to signify that the head was sacred.

Dressing Down

If you're so successful that you don't have to look it, and you wear

- $4,000 simple leather jackets flung casually over a torn T-shirt

- $100 ripped jeans from Fred Segal

- $500 used Levi jackets from trendy boutiques

- $3,000 "distressed" cowboy boots

you're into dressing down.

"Dressing down" is an interesting fashion phenomenon that has developed over the last decade or so as a response to success. The practice has become especially popular among artists and celebrities. In fact, dressing down is now considered a tangible badge of accomplishment. It's a way to show that you've become so successful, you've got nothing left to prove.

In a way, the successful person who dresses down "plays the role" of a not-so-successful person; on the other hand, there's a definite status attached to dressing ultracasual—even drab! Today, many of Hollywood's elite consider it chic to be dowdy. Such celebrities appear to be conveying that they are not at all concerned with fashion; in fact, however, they spend an extraordinary amount of time—and money—cultivating their "downtrodden renegade" look.

Then there are those successful women who dress down to express their newfound confidence. No longer needing to prove themselves professionally, they throw away the dress-for-success uniform and adopt a more unconventional look. Since the dressed-up style symbolizes their struggling days, they develop a disdain for it and often go to the opposite extreme.

What the wearer says when she shows up at a black-tie affair in T-shirt, jeans, leather jacket, and cowboy boots is, "I have nothing to prove anymore. I've made it, and I can dress however I please." Dressing down can turn into an affront, however, when it is practiced at inappropriate times.

If you feel you've earned the right to "dress down," be aware that others may be sensitive about your showing up to their formal gathering in clothes they'd never leave the house in.

BOHEMIAN BABES

If your closet contains four out of five of these items . . .

- black long-sleeved turtleneck T-shirt or sweater

- black skirt or slacks

- black tights

◆ black shoes

◆ beret (black or dark, muted color)

you're unquestionably a bohemian babe!
The artistic bohemian look sprang forth in the nineteenth century when the anti-Establishment "bohemians" wanted to distance themselves from middle-class values. (The word *bohemian* is derived from the French word for Gypsies, who have always remained on the periphery of capitalist society.) Today, the bohemian look expresses a thirst for the intellectual, artistic, exotic life.

The color black is integral to the bohemian look, having infiltrated the world of literature and jazz in post–World War I Paris and becoming very popular among Left Bank intellectuals. Black does not distract from the artist's palette and allows creative people a kind of blank slate from which to draw inspiration. Parisian bohemians also expressed their disdain for bourgeois society by wearing black turtlenecks, tights, and heavy black eye makeup, the bohemian dancer's uniform.

Many still take on this dark look to express an artistic sensibility or a contempt for wealth and middle-class mores. The classic black turtleneck lends a haunting air to the wearer and makes her features appear stark. It also draws attention to her face and expression, be it creative, dreamy, or rebellious.

WORKING-CLASS PANACHE

If you favor such blue-collar styles as

◆ overalls with T-shirts or tank tops

◆ thick, rubber-soled canvas work shoes

- heavy wool plaid "lumberjack" shirts and jeans

- khaki "grease monkey" jumpsuits

- bib-front dresses

you're a working-class girl at heart.

Fascination with the look of the blue-collar worker is an attempt, conscious or not, to get in touch with the gestalt of the American laborer. There's an honorable virility associated with the working class, since its members embody the physical work ethic that our society professes to admire. It's no wonder this is a quality many of us wish to emulate.

When a woman wears denim workshirts, overalls, mechanic's jumpsuits, or wool plaid lumberjack shirts, she conjures up romantic notions of sacrifice and dedication associated with physical endeavors. Overalls, for example—functional and durable—were the classic uniform for many blue-collar workers, including farmers and early twentieth-century factory workers. Today they're available in fashion colors from peach to mauve.

Inspirational figures for tough guy worker chic include muscular, hard-hatted construction workers in ribbed tanks and faded jeans; farmers working in the scorching fields in their faded overalls; mechanics sliding under cars in grease-stained jumpsuits; and hearty outdoorsmen, chopping wood in plaid shirt and faded jeans.

Today, the simple satisfaction of physical accomplishment is often lost in the morass of electronics and mass production. Blue-collar dressing is a superficial way to escape our automated society and pay homage to the world of physical labor. A woman who chooses to adorn herself in the aura of the worker may also feel a vicarious sense of masculine brawn.

DRESS CODE

THE HIPPIE

If your inner hippie loves to wear

- flat, open-toed leather sandals

- anything Native American

- hand-embroidered peasant blouses and full peasant skirts

- long strands of colorful beads

- macramé belts

- anything paisley

- bell-bottom pants with sleeveless tunics

- anything fashioned from fabric that looks like the American flag

- feathers or tiny bells around your neck

- flowers in your hair

face it, you're part of the love generation.

The hippie revolution erupted in the 1960s as a protest against everything middle class. Thousands of young people flung off the clothing and attitudes of the mainstream, adopting a style that was the antithesis of society's rigid dress codes. Long, flowing, flowered skirts countered conventional tight, narrow ones. Floral paisley and ethnic patterns replaced solid colors. Bright, vivid hues

supplanted subdued, muted shades. Pants flared and became bell-bottoms. Flowing scarves, headbands, and bandannas embraced heads and necks.

Although certain designers, such as Mary Quant (who introduced floor-length vest dresses) and Yves Saint Laurent (who invented the "rich hippie peasant look" using extravagant fabrics), caught the hippie fever, authentic hippies refused to wear mass-produced clothing, preferring to express their individuality by coming up with original outfits pieced together with craftwork, exotic accessories, and army surplus. Often clothes were handmade, recycled, or bought from secondhand stores as a protest against capitalism and waste. Handcrafted touches such as embroidery, macramé, tie-dye, and batik were also popular—as were natural fabrics that let the skin "breathe."

Those who adhere to the hippie philosophy today loathe the idea of wearing the conservative "uniforms" of the business world. Instead they they pay homage to their 1960s and 1970s counterparts and let their imaginations run wild—creating a style that is colorful, comfortable, and often reflective of Native American and Third World cultures.

A woman who dresses in hippie attire may yearn to forsake today's fast-paced, impersonal world for a more natural or communal lifestyle. Wearing such styles signifies rebellion against status, money, and anything that represents the Establishment. The preference is for handmade rather than couture, secondhand store finds, as opposed to pricey boutique fashions.

IMMIGRANT GYPSY CHIC

If the fashions that make your heart sing include

- ◆ contrasting floral print skirts and blouses

- ◆ layers of clothing that look mismatched

- ◆ kerchiefs tied under the neck

- ◆ gold loop earrings

- ◆ colorful fringed shawls

you love to bring out the gypsy in you.

An offshoot of the hippie look is the flamboyant gypsy image. Gypsies are associated with free-spiritedness and an open-minded attitude toward life and possessions. Their romantic, nomadic lifestyle appealed greatly to the nonconformists of the 1960s and 1970s who scorned their parents' cloyingly boring lives.

Peasants and gypsies are known for their colorful rags and layers of natural fabrics, including gauze, cottons, and burlap. Babushkas shroud the heads of the women. Their garments are often amorphous shapes held together by an odd pin and comprise articles that don't seem to match or go together.

When we take on this loose, gypsy style, we exude a certain relaxed, unrestrained earthiness.

PUNK ROCKERS

If you enjoy shocking onlookers with

◆ torn T-shirts

◆ dark eye makeup

◆ fluorescent hair color, spiked hairdos

◆ heavy black leather boots

◆ safety pins and other sharp objects pinned to your garments

◆ lots of zippers, chains, and metal studs

you're in sync with punk.

The punk movement and the fashions it engendered came out of the English working class. The youths of this segment of society felt hopelessly imprisoned in a bleak world over which they had no control. In a shrinking economy, their futures looked dim and their options limited. The outrageous style many young people adopted was an attempt to keep themselves on the outskirts of a society that had handed them a raw deal. Punk gave them a way to fight back, and they took action by dressing offensively. American teenagers soon followed suit.

Even punk gets swept into the mainstream. The eccentric English designer Vivienne Westwood nurtured it by opening a shop that changed its name three times—first Too Fast to Live, then Too Young to Die, and finally Sex and Seditionaries. (Not surprisingly, a seditionary is one who seduces people into revolt.) And punk made it to the silver screen as well. Punk dressing and the punk way of life was best portrayed in the movie *Sid and Nancy*, based on the life of Sid Vicious (of the punk rock group the Sex Pistols) and his girlfriend Nancy. Throughout the film Vicious was seen wearing ripped black denim jeans and studded jackets. Nancy was outfitted in either skintight jeans and T-shirts or leather miniskirts with black leather corsets and ripped stockings held up by visible garters. Together, the couple epitomized the gritty, violent world of punk.

Like the punk rock look, many antifashion styles are descendants of the music scene. Designer translations of such antifashion influences include Jean Paul Gaultier, who reportedly culls inspiration from rock music, and Stephen Sprouse, who originally launched ready-to-wear fashions taken from rocker rags with peace signs and graffiti-sprawled T-shirts. Sunset Strip in Los Angeles is a mecca for new bands, and a distinct subculture of antifashion has emerged from this scene. Every weekend thousands of female rock groupies exude sexuality, desperation, and rebellion in such clothing choices as black leather bras, fishnet stockings and high heels, and biker jackets. Striving for a defiant yet glamorous lifestyle, they then set the pace not only for the generation behind them but for designers who look to such fashionable "scenes" for creative ideas.

Punk attire is intended to incite a shocking, negative reaction. The woman who takes her fashion cues from the punks appears to be expressing either her strong contempt for society or a sense of self-deprecation or even self-abuse. She also conveys that she needs attention, even if it is negative. On the other hand, it's possible to wear specific articles of punk attire for dramatic effect or to modify the look to your own specifications. Such would be appropriate for a wild party or ultracasual social occasion.

COWGIRL FLAIR

If you can't wait to fling off your work clothes and don

- rhinestone-encrusted chambray or denim shirts

- conch belts with silver and turquoise

- embossed leather cowboy boots

- flounce skirts

- suede vests

- saloon-style silk vests with buckles in back

- denim jackets with cutoff sleeves

- tooled leather belts

- bandannas

- suede or leather jackets with fringe

- bolo ties

◆ ruffled petticoats over chaps

◆ a ten-gallon hat

you know you're an urban cowgirl.
With its raunchy, unsophisticated sex appeal, cowboy/cowgirl garb has always been antifashion. Cowgirls are perceived as tough yet tantalizing, with heroines such as Kitty Russell in *Gunsmoke* and Annie Oakley in *Annie Get Your Gun* reinforcing that image.

In *Bad Girls,* starring Madeleine Stowe and Andie MacDowell, a more contemporary celluloid depiction of this Wild West archetype shows cowgirls being more like cowboys.

As we approach the twenty-first century, cowboy boots, chaps, and prairie skirts allow us vicariously to experience that gritty, freewheeling feeling of our western foremothers. Cowboy/cowgirl culture represents independence, strength, and ruggedness. Dressed in authentic western gear—blue jeans, long-sleeved western shirts, and cowboy boots with heels designed to stay in the stirrups—you'll appear able to whoop it up with the guys. Cowgirl dresses and skirts merge the rugged with the feminine and convey a sense of sexy, "macha" energy.

MILITARY WEAR

If you love to stand at attention in

◆ military jackets with brass buttons and stripes on stiffly padded shoulders

◆ navy military capes worn over a navy dress or skirt

◆ khaki army fatigues with clunky boots

. . . military fashion is your passion.

Military uniforms, camouflage fatigues, and army jackets endow women with a feeling of power and bravado. They're also a sign of courage, since these are the clothes worn in combat. Military-inspired jackets with braids, medals, brass buttons, and epaulets represent the fashion industry's attempt to capitalize on the consumer's need to emulate heroism. Women who wear combat fashions project a sense of dominance and authority, but if carried to an extreme and worn exclusively, this style might reflect inner turbulence or a sense that the wearer is at war with society and its dictates.

RAPPER RAGS

If you dig playing the hip-hop role in

- a gas station attendant's uniform

- baggy pants (If you want to be really authentic, they must be baggy enough to reveal your underwear underneath.)

- a baseball caps worn backwards

- hip-hop rhinestone caps

- big gold medallions hanging from a chain around your neck

you're into rapper rags.

Like rock 'n' roll before it, rap music and hip-hop have spurred their own genre of rebellious dressing. Such funky garments, inspired by actual street styles, are an attempt to get in touch with the authenticity of inner-city life. Rap fashion gained wide appeal when the rap group Public Enemy took its message of black pride to the airwaves, enjoyed enormous popularity, and saw its style become enmeshed in mainstream popular culture.

Most women over thirty would look pretty silly wearing this very youthful style, but, again, certain elements can be adapted to create a more sophisticated, modified hip-hop look.

EQUESTRIAN STATUS

If you yearn to play out your equestrian fantasies in

- hacking jackets

- riding pants with suede knee patches

- jodhpurs

- Hermès scarves

- jockey caps

- riding boots

consider yourself part of the horsey set.

In recent years, equestrian clothes and paraphernalia have been a ubiquitous fashion trend, deriving from the traditional dress of the hunt. Whether or not we feel at home in the stable, dressing as if we do lends an athletic elegance to our outward appearance.

For many women the equestrian theme is a pleasant reminder of childhood, when they were enthralled with everything that had to do with horses.

As adults, the casual sophistication and slenderizing effect of riding jackets, jodhpurs, and riding boots allow us to feel stylishly attached to the equestrian culture, a world pervaded with an aura of sophistication, old money, social standing, and leisure-time accomplishments.

The older the riding boots and clothes, the more status attached to them; their well-used appearance imply that a woman has had these items a long time and therefore is not a newcomer to the equestrian world. Equestrian styles also convey the sense that the wearer is a "lady of leisure" who is able to spend her time riding rather than working.

Women who choose equestrian fashion take on the best of two worlds: the ruggedness and athleticism of horseback riding and the genteel, cultured ambience of upper-class life. Jacqueline Kennedy Onassis and Princess Di represent the classic embodiment of this type of elegant sportswoman.

Take care that you "role-play" in this style only for very sporty, casual occasions. Showing up in the conference room in jodhpurs and riding boots would definitely not constitute a class act.

ANCHORS AWAY

If you'd love to sail away in

- ◆ navy-blue-and-white-striped T-shirts with white cotton ducks or shorts

- ◆ simple blue or white canvas shoes

- ◆ yachting caps

- admiral-type navy blue blazers with brass buttons—and perhaps gold officer stripes encircling the cuff

- white linen or flannel trousers with a red, white, or navy blazer

- sun visors or sailor caps

you were meant for nautical chic.

Nautical wear also speaks of leisure pursuits (particularly yachting and sailing) and is an obvious symbol of the upper-class lifestyle. Options run the gamut from flirty sailor suits to tailored nautical blazers. Again, the image combines fitness and privilege—and there's a certain fresh quality one takes on as well when wearing the crisp blue-and-white color scheme inherent in these fashions. One need not sail the seas in order to take advantage of this becoming look; it is quite appropriate for any casual occasion.

THE BODY BEAUTIFUL

If you love to get physical in

- plush warm-up suits in every color of the rainbow

- a clean white pair of Reebok, Nike, or other recognized-brand athletic footwear

- crisp white tennis dresses

- silky or cotton running shorts with tank tops to match

you're a natural in the athletic look.

A well-toned physique, or at least the appearance of one, is highly desirable in today's society. Wearing status leisure clothes, nautical wear, dance clothing, jogging togs, and other athletic wear has emerged as a way to convey to others our physical strength. Such clothing signifies that we pursue an active, not sedentary, lifestyle.

If we go out to lunch in a cashmere polo shirt, jeans, and a sweater tied around our necks, or are seen toting tennis gear down a busy urban street, we are implying that our athletic interests are so important to us that we never quite leave them behind.

How many times have you seen a woman in an expensive Tacchini warm-up suit with freshly sprayed beauty parlor hair, perfect makeup, and expensive jewelry? This woman is not about to sweat or muss her hair, yet she wants to be thought of as the athletic type, as someone is likely to dash out of an important meeting for a quick set of tennis on a moment's notice. She may not be physically fit, but her clothing announces that fitness is a priority with her.

Many of us want to look as if we are athletic, even if the very thought of exercise exhausts us! Certainly the image we convey is a robust, healthy one—provided we forgo the heavy makeup and overly lacquered hair. Who knows, perhaps wearing the outfits and "role-playing" the athlete might ultimately inspire us to get out there and sweat!

Chapter 8

Shoe Passions: The Bottom Line on Footwear

"Can you recall a woman who ever showed you with pride her library?"

—de Cassares

A well-known author living in San Francisco walks into a shoe store and drops $100,000 without trying on a single shoe. "She just buys several pairs in different colors. She makes it so easy," gushed the ecstatic salesperson. Though few of us are able to indulge our passion for footwear in a similarly extravagant fashion, it's clear that, for many, shopping for shoes is more than an annual back-to-school chore. Perhaps no other item we put on says more about us—or sends as potent a message—as our shoes. And we're willing to pay the price to make certain our feet are expressive and well heeled. In 1992 the footwear industry's annual sales topped $7 billion.

This preoccupation with shoes is nothing new. Empress Josephine, the much envied wife of Napoléon, was a keen follower of shoe and dress fashions. She was known to change her clothing and shoes four or five times each day, blithely discarding a pair of shoes after a single wearing. Marie Antoinette also owned an abundance of shoes, which she cataloged by color and style, thus ensuring she would never be glimpsed in the same pair twice in a row. It's said she possessed some shoes so delicate that they could be worn only when she was seated.

Today, influential women in all fields succumb to this passion for shoes. In 1987, *W* reported that the late Diana Vreeland owned 125 pairs of custom-made shoes and boots; while *Vogue* magazine revealed that art dealer Mary Boon "keeps her extensive shoe collection, including 225 pairs by Susan Bennis and Warren Edwards, archived in their original boxes." And who could forget Imelda Marcos's infamous collection of shoes, said to be more than 3,000 pairs strong?

Why is so much attention directed to what we put on our feet? What compels women to adorn this seemingly ignoble body part so extravagantly?

THE FOOT IS A SEXUAL ZONE

The foot is an erotic and sensual body part, with a life and shape all its own. Not only can the feet be a source of sexual arousal, they are the culmination of another highly erotic zone, the legs.

If someone at a party asked you to remove your shoes and stockings, your first reaction would likely be one of embarrassment or even humiliation. Why? Because exposing the foot is almost as personal as exposing the breast. Both have cleavage. Being barefoot is akin to being naked, and many of us equate kicking off our shoes with disrobing. This casual gesture also has a not-so-subconscious meaning. When one removes her shoes, it intimates there is more to come.

The pairing of the foot and the shoe is deeply sexual. An ancient theory, over ten thousand years old and still widely held, posits that the simple act of slipping one's foot into a shoe re-creates the sexual act. More recently, Freud postulated that a woman's shoe is emblematic of her vagina.

In William B. Rossi's book *The Sex Life of the Foot and Shoe,* Robert Riley, a design consultant at the Brooklyn Museum and an authority on the history of clothing, talks about the big toe as a phallic symbol and the area between a woman's toes being symbolic of cleavage. He goes on to say that when the foot is thrust into the shoe, this is emblematic of the sex act.

The sexual mystique of a woman's feet and shoes is poetically revealed in the story of Cinderella. When the Prince comes searching for the woman whose unique foot size will fit the glass slipper, this part of Cinderella's body becomes the main focus of the narrative. The slipper is small and dainty—just like Cinderella's foot—and symbolizes the fragile, virginal qualities she embodies. Of course, these are the very traits the Prince hopes to find in a future wife. When he finally slips the glass slipper on Cinderella's foot, this act signifies the impending loss of Cinderella's virginity.

In ancient China, the practice of foot binding also contained an erotic element. The Chinese worshiped "the lotus" or "lily foot," and this deformity of the foot, whether from foot binding or other means, created an aura of eroticism (although even then many found it cruel). Bound feet measured as little as four inches long and were thought to symbolize the male genitals. The Chinese considered the bound foot aristocratic and at once childlike and erotic. Women with bound feet were said to have a unique sexual power over men, who regarded them as goddesses. Many men would make love to the lotus foot before making love to the woman herself.

Even in contemporary times there are painful drawbacks—physical and emotional—attached to glamorous feet. Constrictive shoes, such as stilletto-heeled pumps, force a woman to take small, mincing steps; and such styles not only make her appear tentative, passive, and dependent but hurt her feet if worn for any length of time. Although we may be far removed from the inhumane practices of ancient China, many of us still sacrifice comfort for sex appeal.

A WALK THROUGH THE DECADES

In addition to their sexual symbolism, shoes are also a telling barometer of their era. The ornate shoes of the 1920s reflected the gaiety and liberation of that period.

As skirts rose, shoes for the first time became the focal point of an outfit. Exotic fabrics such as lamé, embroidered silk with pearls, and leather appliqué—as well as jeweled buckles—flourished. High-heeled shoes in velvet or silver brocade were designed especially for dancing, and a sudden interest in sports—tennis, golf, sailing, and shooting—gave birth to sporty new styles.

The practical shoes of heavy grained leather that predominated in the 1930s are a reflection of the hard times that prevailed in that era. The main features of these shoes were comfort and durability. When leather became scarce in the wartime 1940s, fabric shoes emerged. The 1950s brought a return to extravagant froufrou heels, a sign of the unliberated woman thrust into the role of complacent housewife and passive sexual object.

A time of outrage, youthquake, and extremes, the 1960s surprised the public with mod and audacious styles—see-through boots that clung to the legs, wet-look patent leather and vinyl, and geometric patterns. The women's movement and "me generation" influences of the 1970s brought such disparate styles as no-nonsense, comfortable Birkenstocks and silly, ego-enhancing shoes like platforms.

Known for its culturally sanctioned overindulgence, the 1980s revived frankly expensive shoes and brought esoteric, high-priced designers out of their exclusive niche and into the public eye.

WHAT'S IN A SHOE?

Our shoes say a lot about us. They can indicate our character, financial and social level, profession, sex, even our age. They offer hints about where we live and our cultural background. Our choice of footwear reflects our personality; they can divulge whether we think of ourselves as daring or distinguished, a conservative or a free spirit. Wearing a particular shoe style is one of the easiest ways to express our emotions. Each style has a soul of its own. Some are sexy, some are earthy, others are sensible at heart. Shoes communicate our desires for a given social status and lifestyle, as well as proclaim our need for power and sex.

Just as a woman might wear a brighter shade of lipstick—or just a slick of gloss—to reflect her mood, so, too, are our shoe choices influenced by our state of mind. When we slip on a distinct type of shoe, to some degree, consciously or not, we adopt its traits. Even forgoing shoes altogether says something. Because the barefooted woman comes in direct contact with the earth, the symbol of fertility and reproduction, she can't help but exude a natural sensuality.

MATERIAL ISSUES

Among other aspects of the shoes we wear, the material from which they're made gives off subtle indications as to our personality, status, and sexuality.

Different leathers exude varying degrees of power. The more

exotic and expensive leathers and animal skins, such as crocodile, lizard, snakeskin, and ostrich, are powerful symbols of both sensuality and success. Tough, thick leathers like those used for making most loafers come across as masculine and brawny, while the same shoes in more fragile crocodile or snakeskin suggest a flashy, extroverted individual. Snakeskin shoes are perhaps the most overtly sexual because of the snake's symbolic connotations; the snake is not only phallic but harkens back to the fall of Eve.

Soft leathers like calf, kidskin, and suede are softly sensual rather than brazenly sexual. They cling to the foot, hugging and sculpting its contours. Highly polished and shiny skins, such as patent leather and crocodile, bespeak a flamboyant exhibitionist, one whose personality may be as grandiose as the polished shine on her shoes.

Rougher skins like steerhide, buckskin, and coarse grainy leathers assert a macho virility and are a vital component of androgynous looks; the stiffer and more indestructible the leather, the more powerful its message. Loafers, pumps, lace-up oxfords, and brogues made of stiff leather make the wearer appear strong and allow her to express the more masculine side of her personality, letting others know that she has her softer side kept well under wraps.

Shoes can also balance or temper the rest of our outfit. For example, a powerful woman at the top of the entertainment or advertising field may finish off her casual outfit of jeans, T-shirt, and blazer with sturdy oxfords or loafers. Such attire is calculated to disarm those she meets. But although she appears to have a sense of humility, the ostrich or crocodile skin of her shoes betray her status in a tangible way. Similarly, the woman in a tailored suit who wears a pair of audacious, animal print pumps subtly reveals that there is another side to her very proper demeanor and hints at a wilder side of her personality.

Our shoes tell others whether we are controlled, reliable, organized, or restrained. Shoes made of durable, tough materials safeguard our emotions and our femininity; there is no fear of their falling apart, and by extension, when we wear them we may be saying that *we* are less likely to fall apart emotionally—at least in public or professional situations. Stiff shoes with thick or rounded soles may also signify defiance of traditional female roles.

THE EIGHT BASIC SHOE GROUPS

Have you ever wondered why you constantly seem to be in need of new shoes—even if last year's half-dozen pairs still have plenty of tread left on them? Like the rest of the fashion business, the shoe industry sees to it that enticing new styles are offered each season to make year-old shoes seem old hat.

There are actually eight fundamental prototypes from which shoe designers create each season's "latest" looks. Every new pair of shoes you buy falls into one of the following basic shoe groups:

◆ Boots Mules

◆ Oxfords Pumps

◆ Clogs Moccasins

◆ Monks Sandals

Of these eight styles, most fall into one of two categories: sexy or sensible.

Sexy	Sensible
Monks	Oxfords
Mules	Clogs
Pumps	Moccasins

Depending on the particular style, boots and sandals can qualify as either sexy or sensible.

Each shoe type has its own historical roots, as well as a distinct encoded message that's sent the minute we slip the shoe on our foot.

A BRIEF HISTORY OF THE SEXY SHOE

No shoe has more erotic impact than those with high heels. It was the diminutive Catherine de' Médici, wife of Henry II, who first helped launch high-heeled shoes into high fashion.

For her wedding to Henry, she had an Italian designer add high heels to her shoes to make her look thinner and taller. It was so effective that women soon clamored for shoes that would do the same for them. Shoemakers all over the continent were swamped with orders for high-heeled shoes, some of which were so slim that the women wearing them required the help of staff to keep them from toppling over.

High heels remained the exclusive province of the aristocracy for years, since such shoes were highly impractical for women who had to perform menial labor (thus the origin of the term *wellheeled*). Madame Kathy, owner of a famous New Orleans brothel, introduced Americans to high heels in the 1880s when one of her girls brought a pair with her from Paris. Walking around Madame Kathy's establishment in the high heels—and very little else—she incited lust in every male visitor and soon became the most desired woman in town. Madame Kathy discovered that by having her girls wear high heels, she could double her fees. Knowing a good thing when she saw one, she commissioned a Parisian artist to design high-heeled shoes for her to sell through her brothel! Men who patronized her establishment were soon buying these shoes for their wives and girl-friends. It wasn't long before the first American factory began pro-duction of the now classic high heel.

Fashion forefather Count Alfred Guillame Gabriel d'Orsay, a con-tinental dandy, created the d'Orsay pump in the nineteenth century. This shoe dips to a low curve on each side, exposing the arch while accentuating the movement of the foot. This design makes thin legs appear more curved, thick legs look more slender, and short legs seem longer visually—and still exudes a strong sense of sexuality today.

Another blatantly erotic style is the poulaine, a pointed toe or slipper with a furry pom-pom. Men wore them as early as the eleventh century, stuffing the upturned toes with moss to keep them erect and then using them to titillate women under the dining table by lifting the hems of their skirts. Just looking at these infamous shoes, one senses their strong male/female symbolism; the pointed, hornlike shape is very phallic, and the round pom-poms suggest female anatomy. This scandalous, brazen shoe was even known to produce orgasms. (One pair of poulaines in the collection of a con-temporary Italian shoe manufacturer is dubbed the "self-sufficient sexual shoe.") This type of poulaine had a high-rise tongue, resem-bling the phallus, that curved back and joined or buried the tongue tip in fur, leaving much to the imagination. Today the modified poulaine, with its exaggerated, pointed, or squared-off toe, enjoys considerable popularity.

While its name and origin are quite incongruous with its reputa-tion, the pilgrim or monk shoe is a purely erotic fashion item. It evolved from shoes worn in European monasteries during the fif-teenth century, and to this day there is more than a bit of irony in a woman wearing this symbol of the prototypically repressed male. With its long tongue and slim, low-cut shape, this shoe is extremely phallic and suggestive. A strap that reaches to the side of the ankle and fastens with an ornate buckle compresses the foot like a corset, slenderizing and tapering the foot's appearance.

A sexy shoe parallels the silhouette of a woman's body. Adding a bow to the back gives the illusion of a bustled female form bending down. Placing a bow or trim at the front of the shoe is like decorating the breasts. Shoes with jewels, diamonds, and emeralds creeping sinuously up the heels were the original seventeenth-century come-hithers. Cutouts or peepholes at the back of the shoe revealed a tantalizing bit of skin. Today, come-hither shoes include sling-back heels, backless shoes with heels that curve the calf, and pointed, low-cut high-heeled pumps.

Shoe designer Roger Vivier ushered in the stiletto or needle heel in 1953 and aptly named it the "shock heel." Shock heels elevated some of Hollywood's most famous sex symbols, including Jayne Mansfield and Anita Ekberg, and stiletto shoes figure prominently in foot fetishes. They often come in black patent leather with hardware accoutrements, like silver zippers.

Though far less revealing, the over-the-knee boot also has extreme sexual connotations and is associated specifically with sadomasochism. During the 1965 raid of the infamous brothel known as Monique's House of Torture, an enormous collection of knee-high and hip-high boots were discovered.

WHY SEXY SHOES ARE SO SEXY

A woman's feet may be immune to the inhibitions that otherwise govern her clothing choices. By pairing a demure black dress with sexy shoes, she can communicate that she wants to be viewed as a desirable woman without resorting to overtly erotic clothes that she finds too threatening. A soft leather or kidskin shoe can achieve this effect because of the way it silhouettes the foot, highlighting every curve and subtly turning the foot into a sex object.

Soft leather, lizard, kidskin, calf, and crocodile wrap the foot in a sexual embrace. Other styles that exude sensuality are pumps and sandals that lace up the calf or wrap around the ankle, creating a stylized illusion of bondage; strippy sandals; and shoes that expose the "cleavage" of the toes. The sexiest shoes are low-cut, slightly pointed high-heeled pumps with deeply sliced throats that reveal toe cleavage.

High-heeled pumps with pointed toes have a highly sexual effect on a woman's body. By throwing her body out of alignment, they force her to thrust her breasts forward, arch her back slightly, and emphasize her derriere. Her walk becomes transformed into a provocative gesture.

High heels capture the male eye and draw his attention to the back of our leg. Shoes that beckon the eye up the leg are the most alluring, enticing the man to follow the line of the leg and fantasize about the end of his visual journey.

High heels also contour the instep and arch. When they are severely tapered, they hug and slenderize the foot and imbue the wearer with that vulnerable, mincing walk men find so appealing. High heels with ankle straps or ribbons that wind up the leg carry with them subtle references to bondage; when we wear them, we hint that we may enjoy being restricted or constrained.

An old Chinese adage held that high-heels cause blood to flow faster in the female genitals, arousing women quickly. This myth persists even today. Men believe that heels heighten sexual arousal in women because of the suggestive posture her body assumes when she wears them. And, of course, men find the very thought of women in high heels erotic. This may in part be due to the fact that high

heels make women appear helpless and in need of men for support.
A man's pleasure derives not only from knowing that a woman is
looking to him for help, but that she is consciously dressing provocatively to arouse him.

There is also a masochistic element to high heels, which can be
quite painful to wear. Yet for some, the pleasure of knowing that

their shoes trigger a sexual response in men makes up for any discomfort caused.

Passive Sexy Shoes	**Aggressive Sexy Shoes**
◆ High-heeled stiletto soft pumps	◆ Over-the-knee boots in kidskin, snakeskin, or patent leather
◆ Manolo Blahnik shoe with tapered shape and thin heel	◆ Robert Clergerie or Philip Model shoes with sturdy rounded or squared front and thick chunky, curved, or molded heels

PLATFORMS—SCALING THE HEIGHTS

Everyone from flower children in the 1960s to runway models in the
1990s has adopted the platform to raise fashion—as well as their
own personal stature—to soaring heights. Women feel that added
height slenderizes them, makes them feel powerful, and contributes
to their sense of confidence.

However, because platforms can be treacherous for walking or
being physically active, this effect is undermined by a secondary
message of helplessness. Despite their illusion of height and power,
platforms are ultimately associated with passivity.

Often made of cork, rope, or wood, platforms range from the
relatively minute to skyscraping proportions. They found their
place in society over 3,500 years ago, when they were used in the

Greek theater to indicate the importance of an actor's role. Royals have had platforms put in their shoes for centuries. Chopines, wooden, stiltlike footwear that added up to thirty inches in height, originated in the East and were used by women for hygienic reasons when visiting the public baths. In the early sixteenth century they became quite popular in Venice, Italy. In Syria, contemporary brides get married in platform clogs called kubbabs, which may be as high as twelve inches—making brides appear imposing but unfortunately denying them freedom of movement.

Despite their regal origins, platforms have their scandalous side as well. Women in Arabian harems wore platforms, as did Japanese courtesans, who displayed them as an emblem of their profession. Other women of disreputable means were marked by the wearing of platform shoes in the red-light district in Rome.

In 1936, high-fashion czar Ferragamo reinvented his infamous platform when a shortage of Italian steel prevented him from producing his famous stiletto heels. Without steel to support the arch, the shoe would collapse. His ingenious alternative was a cork wedge or platform in multicolored layers of ropelike braiding, with metallic

gold straps that served the same purpose and ushered in a new fashion trend.

Carmen Miranda wore a lively collection of platforms in her 1940s films, making them quite popular among women of that era.

The dangers of platforms probably outweigh any possible distinguishing benefits. Both the American Medical Association and the Podiatry Safety Council have issued warnings about platforms, and when a pregnant woman in Venice, Italy, fell wearing platforms and subsequently miscarried, that city passed a law prohibiting the wearing of them.

MULES AND THONGS

The mule, with or without an open toe, is quite simply a flirtatious shoe. Not as intensely erotic as stiletto or thin high-heeled pumps, mules leave the back of the foot exposed, curving the calf and directing attention to the back of the leg. However, the completely covered front keeps them from coming on too strong.

The mule is basically a slipper and—until the Italians stuck a heel on it—was an indoor shoe worn originally by the ancient Sumerians. Fashion-conscious ladies of leisure and courtesans wore mules as bedroom slippers. Mules were the shoe of choice for Japanese courtesans as well as for women in Arab harems. Not surprisingly, the heel on the shoe symbolizes putting a woman on a pedestal. Because mules are impractical and coquettish, they make it impossible for a woman wearing them to do much; she cannot walk quickly in them, and taking stairs is tricky. Such limitations imply that a woman who wears mules has a lot of time on her hands. If they are expensive and jewel encrusted, mules speak of leisure and money.

Like a partially clothed woman, mules reveal and conceal at the same time. They are innocently sexual because they invite one to imagine what lies hidden. Mulelike boots, which mask the front while softly lacing up the naked back, are equally flirtatious. The lacing adds an element of sexual game playing.

In the golden age of Hollywood, mules (usually satin) served as a kind of sexual trademark for such stars as Jayne Mansfield and Marilyn Monroe and figured prominently in their film roles. In *The Seven Year Itch,* Monroe frequently wore mules with feathers and furs. Then, for no apparent reason, mules with feathers, furs, and rhinestones largely disappeared—until designer Manolo Blahnik updated and repopularized them.

Like mules, thongs are ill suited to all but the most leisurely pursuits and have a similarly sensual appeal. Thongs date back to ancient Roman times, when they were the traditional footwear of prostitutes. Since any form of nudity was unacceptable in proper society, sandals or slippers that bared the skin were very risqué.

SENSIBLE SHOES

An eligible bachelor—whose succession of women and sexual exploits make Don Juan look like an amateur—was once being

interviewed on a talk show. He lamented that he could not find the right woman.

"What are you looking for?" inquired the host.

"I just want a Berkeley-esque woman. You know, long, flowered dresses and Birkenstocks."

"Birkenstocks?" inquired the host with surprise.

"Yes, you know, the funny-looking sandals. They're the sign of a down-to-earth woman. The shoe that signals a woman really has two feet on the ground."

Because she is unwilling to endure the discomfort of sexy shoes, the woman who opts for earthy shoes appears practical and sensible. Others sense her lack of pretension and see her as open and approachable.

Sensible shoes may not be sexual, but they can be sensual. The foot is made to feel comfortable, and the wearer is at ease with and in touch with her world. Comfortable shoes literally keep a woman's feet on the ground.

Oxfords, sneakers, earth shoes, Birkenstocks, and ballet slippers fit the foot comfortably and adhere to its natural contour. When we wear this type of shoe, we communicate to others that we're pragmatic, reliable, and stable. Sensible shoes are modest and durable, so the woman who wears them seems trustworthy and capable of sustaining a relationship.

The Birkenstock is a German design first introduced in the United States in the late sixties by American Margot Fraser, a former dress designer. Fraser, sick of pinched, tired feet, discovered Birkenstocks while in Germany. When she returned to the United States, she looked into importing the shoes and ultimately became the sole distributor in the United States. Dubbed "hippie gear" in Berkeley, they were initially regarded as peculiar sandals with contoured footbeds. Today they are available in over 125 styles and have become so out, they're in.

Another sensible shoe is the oxford, which takes its name from Oxford University in England, where students rebelled against the discomfort of ankle and knee-high boots. As a compromise, the school offered the option of a low-cut laced shoe that came to be known as the oxford. The oxford's collegiate appearance makes the woman wearing them seem both youthful and intellectual.

Though sturdy, these shoes have a beauty all their own. The laces of the oxford narrow and slenderize the foot, making it appear girlish. A popular favorite is the two-toned spectator oxford or the suede oxford. If made of a stiff material, they suggest a serious, dependable woman, disciplined in thought.

Brogues resemble the oxford in shape and are either laced or have a T-strap. They were worn by gamekeepers in England, who needed a shoe that would hold up in any weather. Perforated to allow any water that might seep into the shoe to drain out, brogues gained social status from their association with the aristocratic men who wore them to the hunt; genteel women wore the stiff yet elegant brogue for leisurely country pursuits. These shoes convey an aura of affluence and elevated social standing.

Spectators, shoes that combine dark and light leathers, found their place in society during the 1920s and 1930s. They reflected the inter-marriage of black and white music. Oxford or pump spectators are still fashionable today. The shoe's inherent contrasts say the wearer is an extrovert, yet somewhat arrogant and not very open with her feelings.

The moccasin, one of the earliest known shoe styles, has been around for almost six thousand years. The earliest version was a simple piece of hide that covered the foot. Although not a serious shoe, the moccasin is the blueprint for all slip-on shoes, such as loafers, flats, and pumps, sensible shoes all.

Ballet shoes are the most minimal form of footwear. Although women have been wearing them for over two hundred years, Capezio first introduced flat "ballet pumps" in the 1940s, when Claire

McCardell resurrected them for street wear. In the 1960s, designers Betsey Johnson, Emanuelle Kahn, and Mary Quant eased women out of the stiletto heels that were so popular and revised the ballet pump, the one that was used for ballroom dancing in the nineteenth century, by lowering the heel even farther, making it easier to move in the shoes. Their comfort, practicality, and femininity ensures the ballet slipper's continued popularity.

Clogs are a less glamorous form of platforms, but because they're easy to walk in, clogs qualify as sensible shoes, while platforms do not. The clog originated in the sixteenth century and was favored by workers and country dwellers in Europe. In more recent times, fashion magazines have deemphasized the working-class origins of clogs by featuring them on expensively dressed models. This attempt to lend clogs an air of glamour ultimately failed. Clogs may be fashionable and lend a woman height, but they're not glamorous. They remain largely the province of teenagers, college girls, and gardeners.

THE MASCULINE FOOT

Masculine shoes fall into the "sensible" category but send a unique fashion message. When we wear masculine-style shoes and boots, we convey a sense of strength and androgyny with erotic overtones.

Such styles often have bulbous toes and thick soles and come in solid leathers. They may have large silver buckles or other decorative hardware. Styles usually worn by men, such as wing-tips, have been adapted for women in times of political and social upheaval both in the 1960s and again in the 1990s. They masculinize a woman's gait, neutralizing her femininity.

♦ The motorcycle boot melds utilitarian footwear with features of the more refined and aristocratic riding boot. It is extremely aggressive and compensates for its lack of sensuality with raw power. Made of hard, sturdy leather, the motorcycle boot is often adorned with silver hardware, buckles, studs, and heavy straps. It has a menacing presence, yet its sturdiness imbues the foot with reliability and strength. The woman in motorcycle boots flouts her femaleness and rebels against the cultural limitations of womanhood.

♦ Slipping on a pair of cowboy boots, we slip into the spirit of the West and take on the virile, rugged qualities of the mythic cowboy. With its pointed toe and high heel, the cowboy boot has an aggressive eroticism. Cowboys possess their own unique charisma: tough, friendly, yet sexual. And by wearing their boots, we can feel a bit of their adventurousness ourselves. Others often perceive a woman in cowboy boots as bold, spirited, and "macha."

♦ Combat or military boots, on the other hand, signify a sense of struggle and strength. They suggest that the wearer may be at war with society or the environment—or herself. A woman who wears such boots on a consistent basis may feel as though her life is a battlefield and is perhaps sending a warning that those around her should be on the defensive.

◆ Rugged, tough hiking and desert boots are also badges of rebellion. These daring yet reliable boots signal dependability. Timberlands, Doc Martens, and Desert Clarkes all have rugged connotations and are particular favorites among social protesters. German-born Klaus Martens created Doc Martens after a skiing accident to make walking less painful—his prototype even included air-conditioned soles. From this came a hiking, walking, and working boot. In the 1960s, these boots were politically correct and often worn in protest marches. They were so popular during the French student revolt that they became an antistatus symbol.

◆ Work boots or hiking boots, such as the chukka boot, declare that the wearer is not only environmentally conscious, but a great believer in outdoor activities. They endow a woman with a natural, athletic virility. Her shoes say that she would rather hike through the woods than tromp through boutiques.

ORNAMENTS

Ornamented shoes provide a decorative form of fantasy and entertainment. Many of us choose festive adornments for evening shoes since they give us a chance to express our lighter side—to have

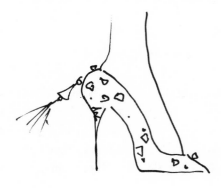

fun, unleash our fantasies. If we're entrenched in corporate America by day, indulging our whims by buying a pair of fanciful evening shoes is a liberating yet harmless antidote to our buttoned-down daytime look.

Ornaments such as bows and pom-poms are usually flirtatious. The bow can add innocence or sexiness, depending on the shoe style and fabric. Bows used to be symbols of power and wealth for men, but on a woman's ankles they are coquettish.

Buckles, bows, spangles, beads, bells, chains, tassels, sequins, jewels, and rhinestones all add status or sex appeal to our shoes. In the eighteenth century, only the very wealthy decorated their shoes with buckles. These status symbols were often encrusted with diamonds and emeralds and were occasionally used on boots in place of buttons. Today, buckles are purely decorative. Delicate buckles add a demure, feminine touch. If the buckle is thick and hard, it might convey a less soft image.

Ornate, sequined shoes suggest a flamboyant lifestyle and spirit. Jeweled shoes are associated with royalty and fantasies. When Princess Diana married, she chose ivory silk shoes adorned with pearls and mother-of-pearl sequins and soles etched in gold.

For his 1977 coronation, Emperor Bokassa of the Central African Republic had a Parisian jeweler custom-make a pair of shoes studded with pearls to match his robe.

IN OUR SHOES

Although shoes are one of the most subtle pieces of the fashion puzzle, they can have an arresting effect. Everything else you're wearing may be perfectly proper, but a daring pair of shoes can hint at an entirely different side of your personality. Shoes provide an interesting and practical way to add distinction to an outfit. In fact, some women rely solely on their shoe wardrobe to punctuate a limited number of garments.

Most of us admit to having a special relationship with our shoes—a closer connection than with any other article of clothing. Maybe it's because our shoes take us where we need to go; they're our transportation, our concrete link to the ground we tread. Or perhaps it's the sensual significance of the foot, rendering whatever covers it sensually meaningful as well. There's nothing like a new pair of shoes to give you that certain lift, nothing as comforting as slipping into a favorite old pair of slippers. Shoes are more than a fashion necessity or statement. For many of us, they're a passion!

SHOE SIGNALS

Shoes to Wear to a Business Meeting

- Crocodile loafers (signals power and status with a sense of groundedness)

- Midheeled conservative pumps (indicates reliability, dignity, and refinement)

- Spectator pumps (conveys power and social standing)

Shoes to Wear to a Formal Black-Tie Affair
(Weddings, Galas . . .)

- Evening pumps in satin silk or velvet (endows the leg with elegance and class and shows respect for the occasion)

- Open-toed sandals that lace up or tie (sends off a flirtatious note, reveals a vulnerable side to the personality)

- Ornamented shoes and pumps (signals that one is ready for an adventurous evening; conveys a flamboyance)

Shoes for Art Openings, Premieres, Screenings,
Book signings . . .

- Ankle boots or lace-up boots (reveals an artistic nature)

- Platforms (signals trendiness)

- Flats (reveals easygoing temperament, fashionable groundedness)

Shoes for the Weekend

- Open-toed sandals (flirtatious in a fun-loving way)

- Sandals with straps (conveys a youthful allure)

- Espadrilles (relaxed nonchalance)

- Cowboy boots (signals a sense of boldness and adventure)

- Riding boots (bespeaks prestige and status)

- Oxfords (signals earthiness, no-nonsense attitude)

Shoes to Wear on Romantic Dates

- Mules (signals that you're open to romance—in a passive, flirtatious sense)

- High-heeled pumps or open-toed sandals (expresses sexuality)

Shoes for the First Date

- Closed pump (shows restraint)

- Flats (expresses casual interest)

Shoes to Wear on a Job Interview

- Midheeled pumps (signifies that you're reliable and have a sense of decorum)

- Interestingly shaped pumps with curved heeled (indicates a creative streak)

Shoes for a Public Appearance/Public Speaking

- Crocodile pumps (adds height and power; elicits respect)

Shoes to Wear to Cocktail Parties or Formal Restaurants

- Black satin high-heeled pumps (they fit in anywhere!)

- High-heeled slingbacks (open and flirtatious)

- Tuxedo flats (relaxed but respectable)

GUIDELINES FOR MAKING SHOE SENSE

Shoes for Business Meetings

Midheeled, conservative pumps are especially proper in real estate, law, executive levels of publishing, and investment banking. Bruno Magli, Bally, and Ferragamo cater to this group of business-minded woman. Practical, low-heeled Ferragamos show that the wearer is polished, reliable, and dignified. In this type of shoe a woman's stride is feminine yet graceful. Such shoes mask sexual communication so that a woman can concentrate on the task at hand.

In creative fields, such as entertainment and fashion, flats work well. They are simple, stylish, and comfortable, and one can create without any physical distraction. In fashion-conscious companies, flats are preferable because they adapt easily to new fashions. People at the higher rungs may flaunt their status by wearing shoes of expensive skins.

Styles at Work

Comfort is a clear priority at work. If you're wearing overly high heels or toes that are too pointy, you may find yourself rushing the meeting or luncheon so you can slip such shoes off your aching feet.

Overly sexy shoes likewise are inappropriate in business settings, as they obviously send the wrong signals. Slingbacks; open-toed sandals, flats, or heels; thongs—

any style that exposes parts of the foot such as the heel or toes—endows the foot with sensuality. Co-workers will have a hard time taking you seriously if you're wearing such styles.

Versatile Shoes

Flats can be worn day or night. In satin or silk they're fine for evening wear. Leather flats work with long skirts, pants, jeans, and leggings. They look best with completely sheer or slightly opaque hose.

Pumps or other shoes with a curved heel can go from day to night. They go well with slim skirts or trousers and should be worn with sheer or opaque hose. Midheel or high-heeled pumps, with or without ornaments, look best with short or long skirts and matching opaque or sheer hose. One can also wear them with trousers.

Casual Occasions

Oxfords and loafers are the perfect style for any casual occasion. They go well with shorts, pants, slim tailored trousers, and jeans. When wearing them with short culottes or skirts, wear opaque or thick, knitted tights. Brogues and spectators look best with long, full skirts, trousers, or jeans.

Shoes sliced open in the front, d'Orsay pumps, and other décolletage shoes should be saved for skirts and suits. Such shoes look awkward with jeans and leggings.

Platforms and clogs can be worn with jeans or

trousers but look inappropriate with skirts and evening wear. Mules look great with shorts and short skirts.

Riding boots look great paired with long, full, or slim skirts. They naturally work well with jodhpurs, jeans, or leggings. Over-the-knee boots should be worn with very short skirts for a vamp effect or with leggings or jeans. Ankle boots can be worn with leggings, trousers, or short skirts with thick tights, but they look awkward with long skirts.

Evening Wear No-no

When a woman rebels by wearing sneakers or work boots with evening wear or ankle socks with pumps, rather than looking chic, she comes across as childish.

Chapter 9

Using Your Head: What Hats and Hairstyles Say

S itting on a salon chair shrouded in a smock, hair plastered damply to her forehead, a woman is perhaps at her most vulnerable. She has put herself in the hands of someone with the power to improve or destroy her looks with a single snip of the scissors.

Our hair is our most prominent—and changeable—feature. And like every other aspect of our appearance, it sends a range of messages, depending on its length, color, texture, and style. Learning which messages are encoded in the particular look we choose for our hair gives us the opportunity to use fashion to our best advantage.

THE POWER OF HAIRSTYLES

Almost as soon as the comb came into common usage, women have been using it to style their tresses for dramatic impact. Coiled braids, chignons, beehives, fluffy, layered hair piled high, and hard lacquered hair have all had their days. Hair has been massed on top of the head, coiled into braids, or sheared into points from outer space à la Marie Antoinette and Madame Pompadour. During the French Revolution and mid-eighteenth century, coifs soared as high as five feet, with the help of wire, wool, horsehair, straw, or false hair. The end result was pasted down, greased, and floured, then adorned with garlands of flowers inspired by rose gardens or theatrical stagings. The coif lasted up to ten days and did more to showcase the creativity of the hairdresser than to enhance the attractiveness of the wearer.

In more recent times, stylized, glamorous, "big hair" has enjoyed a return to vogue. Annette Funicello romped on the beach in her bouffant, while Jacqueline Kennedy crowned hers with a pillbox hat. This high-maintenance style mirrored the times; in the 1950s fewer women held jobs outside the home, and wearing a bouffant implied a woman also had the time to maintain it.

Likewise, the highly teased hair Melanie Griffith sported at the beginning of *Working Girl* bespoke a woman for whom appearance was more important than career protocol; when her character decided to pursue her career more aggressively, she cut and simplified her hairstyle to a shorter, softer, more refined look.

Women used their hairstyles to make a statement of another kind altogether during the French Revolution. In remembrance of those who died at the guillotine (a mode of execution that required its victims be shorn beforehand), aristocrats adopted a new hairstyle appropriately named *à la victime*, a sign of scorn for the executioner. Although this extreme look did not regain a fashion foothold until this century, it was an early example of "liberated hair," styles that do not depend on the hairdresser.

From Twiggy's wispy gamine look to the slightly disheveled Annie Hall effect, liberated styles said, "We refuse to be slaves to the salon—we'd rather do it ourselves." Allowing the wave in one's

hair to show through rather than taming with gels and blow dryers indicated an uninhibited woman comfortable with her true identity.

The nineties seem to be a time when more fashion—including hairdo—options are available to women. Straight, curly, uneven, short, long, natural, stylized—the hairstyle menu is extensive and diverse. Perhaps this means our culture is finally allowing women to be what they want to be, to make choices and changes in appearance according to their own tastes rather than the dicta of the fashion powers-that-be. Gone are the days when a woman had to conform to a single "proper" look in order to be considered "in good taste."

Hair has been a way of projecting social stature for centuries. In the eighteenth century, the French aristocracy placed tremendous importance on coiffures and for centuries dictated what was fashionable. The more hair piled on top of her head, the higher a woman's standing. Curliness and fullness of hair signaled power. No matter how audacious the particular style of the moment, people emulated the hairdos and fashions of the upper crust in order to gain entrée into court society.

In the 1800s, enlisting the services of a hairdresser was a luxury only the wealthy could afford. Ladies of lesser means employed a hairdresser only for special occasions. The elaborate hairstyles of the day bespoke women with no responsibilities other than affecting the proper appearance. Their preoccupation with hairdos and fashions also offered an escape from boredom.

In those days hairdressers came to the home, much like contemporary hairdressers who make house calls to the homes of the very rich. The beauty parlor as we know it today was first launched in the 1870s by Martha Harper, whose Rochester, New York, salon spawned an empire of five hundred shops. More than fifty years later, the first celebrity hairdresser, a Parisian named Antoine, opened a styling salon on the rue de Cambon. A bastion of luxurious sophistication, his salon was responsible for such creations as lacquerlike fixative and blue-dyed hair, popularized in the 1930s by decorator Elsie de Wolfe. Antoine's heir apparent was Alexandra of Paris, whose salon was located a few doors down the street from Chanel. To this day, Alexandra dresses some of the most famous heads in Paris.

The way we wear our hair has always been a barometer of our social values. Poets, artists, beatniks, and hippies sported long, flowing tresses in the 1960s, while more conservative women adopted the tidier, shorter hairdos made popular by Jackie Kennedy and Pat Nixon. African Americans gravitated to the Afro in the late 1960s and cornrows or dreadlocks in the 1970s and 1980s as a way of expressing their cultural roots. Jane Fonda's shag cut in *Klute* did a lot for the American hair salon business.

The high-flying eighties brought high-flying hairdos as well. Big manes of hair became a symbol of power in Hollywood, and top-knots—stiff and sprayed—dominated New York society. The nineties seem to be more grounded in reality, and the key words in hairstyles are "soft" and "touchable."

Today women have an array of distinctive styles from which to choose: short, long, uneven, permed, cropped, colored, and shaved. Of course, we look for haircuts that enhance our features and minimize those we find displeasing, but beauty is only a small part of it. The right hairstyle will communicate our personal attitudes and visually describe our cultural role, as well as frame our face and highlight our features.

THE CONFIDENT CUT

Short, bobbed hair suggests a liberated and powerful woman; she is the mirror opposite of the coy, helpless Rapunzel, who uses her long hair to lure the opposite sex. Short hair widens the face, broadens the jawline, and lifts the cheekbones. The neck becomes prominent, and the chin appears more angular.

In the 1920s, short bobs stood for sexual and professional independence. Women celebrated their right to vote and other newly won social freedoms by renouncing the elaborate pinned-up styles that had confined them for too long. Along with hiked-up skirts and flattened chests, cropped hair illustrated their emancipation. Not surprisingly, many found the bobbed look desexualizing and dubbed women sporting such styles *garconnes,* or "little boys." But soon actress Louise Brooks, in her role as Lulu, made the classic "bob with bangs" both sexually appealing and socially acceptable.

The bob reemerged in the 1960s, when, tired of the chignons her models sported in fashion shows, Mary Quant approached Vidal Sassoon for a new look. He cut the hair into a clean, sharp line with a lot of swing. His five-point geometric cut, feathering around the face and emphasizing the neck, chin, and jawlines, was an immediate hit.

Today, short hair is a sign of self-assuredness. The woman in a short bob appears to be concerned with more than her looks. A shorter cut also implies the woman is more direct, not afraid to bare her features or her soul.

◆ Short hair that is slicked or brushed back conveys a forthright personality.

◆ Short hair and bangs bespeak a more private person, since bangs obscure part of the face.

◆ Slicked-back short hair with one lock of hair that dips seductively over the eyebrow symbolizes androgyny and an erotic playfulness. The woman wearing her hair this way comes across strong yet feminine—the femme element evident in that great lock of sweeping hair.

◆ The short, masculine semi–crew cut, on the other hand, carries militant connotations, since short hair is de rigueur for those in the armed services.

◆ The pixie hairdo that Mia Farrow made famous in *Rosemary's Baby* is sometimes known as "the gamine." This carefree, windswept hairdo washed up from the Italian shores in 1952. Such hairstyles are the sign of a confident woman who faces the world with open features and candid expressions. When you wear your hair this way, you seem to be flaunting your femininity.

Short hair's natural, no-nonsense look has its own sensual appeal—especially since it leaves the neck and ears visible. Since short hair frames your face and draws attention to your eyes—the so-called mirrors of the soul—a short-haired woman comes across as more trustworthy. She seems more open and direct, unafraid to reveal her face or the shape of her head. Short hair is also a sign of discipline and seriousness, which may be why many newscasters keep their hair above their shoulders. When curled or permed, short hair takes on a sassy irreverence.

Widening your eyes and opening your features, short hairstyles lend an air of forthrightness and self-confidence.

LONG LOCKS

When worn loose, long hair is strongly associated with fantasy and sensuality. Long, silky locks conjure up the fairy-tale romance of Rapunzel, while a long mass of Pre-Raphaelite curls implies wantonness. Long hair can also offer a sense of security. We may feel a Sampson-like strength with a full head of hair but must also be aware of the look we're actually projecting.

Long, loose, unrestrained hair has historically carried overt sexual implications. Among the Franks in the Roman Empire, married women wore their red plaited hair in garlands as a sign of their marital status; an old adage held that an unmarried woman *"remant in capillo"* ("remains in her hair"). In Edwardian England, young women pinned up their hair to signal they had reached the age of sexual availability and were ready to offer themselves to a husband. The hair was worn loose on wedding days to indicate their virginity. Once married, a woman cut her hair short as a sign of servitude to her husband. Even today, Orthodox Jewish women don a *shaytl*, or wig, to cover their head after they are married, so that only their husband is allowed to see their hair, considered to be a sexual temptation for other men.

Hair's association with sexual passion goes back as far as the myth of Lorelei, who perched on a rock, crooning her melodies and combing her long golden hair. This enchanting vision caused boatmen to divert their attention from the task at hand, as a consequence of which they lost their lives. More recently, the cinematic image of the schoolmarmish character removing her glasses and shaking out her bun has become a symbol of unleashing female sensuality.

To set free one's hair is to set free one's inhibitions. Men equate loose, untamed hair with a loose, untamed libido. The more elaborate or fantastic a hairdo, the less sexually stirring it is. Restrained, stiff hair suggests a woman whose manner in the bedroom is stiff and restrained as well.

In the sixteenth century, Giovanni Battista Della Porta, a physiognomist, posited that a voluptuous head of hair indicated a woman with carnal hunger. Felix-Alexandre Roubaud, a physician of the same period, noted that an abundance of hair implied a "throbbing libido."

Long hair has always been used to express ideological extremes. In the 1950s, the beatniks in London proclaimed their philosophical open-mindedness by letting their hair straggle around their faces. The flower children of the 1960s rebelled against the stiff, bouffant dos of their parents by wearing their hair wild and natural. And artists and bohemians also wore long hair as a sign of nonconformity.

An abundance of hair has always been a sign of strength; for this reason, male hair loss is often interpreted as a loss of virility. Similarly, long hair on women is associated with vitality and fertility, which may be why some older women continue to wear their hair long, not wanting to relinquish that aura of youthful vigor.

Practically speaking, there are advantages and disadvantages to having long hair. Unless you have a well-shaped haircut, long hair can look messy and ragged. This is especially true the older we get. That is not to say older women cannot wear their hair long, only that they must make certain it is shaped regularly by a professional.

PINNED-UP AND PULLED-BACK STYLES

Pulling back one's hair can be read as pulling back part of one's emotions. A pulled-back style, whether in the shape of a chignon, ponytail, or topknot, implies a certain restraint and reserve. On the other hand, it can create the fantasy of undoing a woman's hairdo, thus liberating her emotions and sexuality. The term *crowning glory* was coined during the Victorian era, when women released their neatly coiffed pompadours only in the privacy of their boudoirs.

Many men continue to perceive upswept hair as a challenge; to unloosen a woman's hair is to cause her to let down her guard, free herself of inhibitions, and open herself sexually. A woman who wears her hair in a sex kitten hairdo may subconsciously be asking for someone to help her completely undo her untidy chignon.

Also, for many the neck is a highly erogenous zone, and upswept styles not only lengthen the neck, but reveal it to onlookers.

The rumpled, tousled, pulled-up look that suggests a woman has just gotten out of bed is especially provocative. When Brigitte Bardot wowed males worldwide in *And God Created Woman,* with her disheveled topknot that now bears names like chignon or twist, women followed her cue. And in the 1990s this look has been resuscitated by model Claudia Schiffer in the seductive Guess ads.

The chignon and its close cousin, the French twist, can be perceived as a coiled phallic symbol. Some of the allure of these looks may derive from a longing to go back to the days before women's liberation—when men were supposed to take care of women. The styles communicate a kittenish, helpless demeanor—which is fine for an evening out with a lover but not appropriate for a business meeting.

Ponytails convey a sense of youthfulness. A ponytail is one of the easiest and most versatile hairstyles. It's also one of the most youthful. Don't most of us remember our mom pulling our hair back into the classic ponytail when we were little? It was neat, quick, and kept us cool on hot days. Chances are those same memories will register with those who see us wearing ponytails as grown-ups. Men will recall their sisters or playmates, and women will go back in time to when this "do" was number one with the playground set.

Still, ponytails don't have to be childish. On adult women, the style can be funky, chic, or conservative, depending on how the ponytail is worn and with what. The higher up the ponytail is on your head, the younger the look. Pulled back loosely at the nape of the neck, it creates a more sophisticated image. And, of course, worn to the side à la Pebbles Flintstone creates a particularly youthful style that should be worn only for play. Nowadays there are lovely ponytail wraps in an array of fabrics and designs that can enhance the ponytail look.

WAVES OF ROMANCE

A most romantic hairdo is wavy hair pinned up with tendrils falling oh so lightly over the face.

Pre-Raphaelite curls with soft tendrils framing a woman's face or veiling her shoulders were popular during the Renaissance. Botticelli's paintings, especially *Venus,* feature waves of hair that float over a woman's body like a seductive covering. Romantic waves again entered the picture in 1872, when the celebrated hairdresser Marcel Grau created his notorious "Marcel wave," which was achieved with the help of a curling iron that crimped the hair into a swerving wave and brought Marcel millions.

This kind of soft, feminine hairstyle can be completely disarming in business situations. It allows a woman to assert herself without fear of seeming too aggressive, because her hair softens her demeanor and renders her less threatening. A short cap of curls, on the other hand, projects a kind of seductive androgyny.

BANGS

Bangs are a focal point that can beautify an array of haircuts. They can make us look younger, since they hide wrinkles; they can bring out our boyish and gamine qualities; or their long wisps can whisper a sexual message. Bangs soften your face and transform a sophisticated style into a less severe one. They add a seductiveness to long hair. Because they cover part of the forehead, bangs draw attention to the eyes. A fringe of bangs lifts the forehead and thins the face. Bangs also shorten long faces.

From a psychological point of view, bangs can also be a form of security—a kind of veil behind which we hide a portion of our face. The current popularity of messy bangs that intentionally fall into the eyes may connote a rebellious aloofness and disrespect for the status quo.

Depending on their length and style, bangs send different messages:

◆ Thick, blunt-cut, broad bangs suggest a more powerful presence since they broaden the face.

◆ Tapered bangs convey an elegance and sophistication.

◆ Very short, blunt bangs suggest a spunky, bold personality.

◆ Wispy bangs with short hair have an innocent yet boyish appeal.

◆ Stiff, sprayed bangs project a tough, controlled image.

◆ Long bangs falling in the eyes send a message of carelessness and seductiveness.

THE LOOK OF POWER

Your attitude, intentions, and work personality are often projected in the hairdo you choose to wear to work.

In business, a neat, well-groomed head of hair suggests strong organizational skills and logical thought. A classic example is the strong cap of hair that is resilient, shiny, smooth, and swings freely. Hairstyles that aren't overtly sexual are obviously more professional, but that doesn't mean you have to look sexless or severe. Hair that flatters the lines of your face and looks natural in texture, cut, and shade will be attractive but not distracting.

Constantly changing your hairstyle may imply that both your personal style and your ideas are still in the process of evolving; sticking to the same look year after year, on the other hand, may convey that you are too set in your ways.

Short, bobbed, or clipped hair that needs little daily maintenance to keep its sharp, powerful shape bespeaks a woman likely found in the executive suite or involved in consuming creative or charitable endeavors. A highly coiffed, elaborate hairdo that requires the support of blowers, curlers, or regular visits to the hairdresser generally signifies a woman more focused on her appearance than on her career; or she runs the risk of suggesting to others that she relies on her image rather than her intelligence to accomplish things.

Hair or bangs that constantly fall in your face detracts from a powerful look. Likewise, overly long or loose hairstyles are inappropriate; they tend to be viewed as too sexy and too playful. Moderation and neatness are key to hairstyle power looks. Short, slicked-back hair is currently a popular power style because it demonstrates that the wearer has the confidence to reveal her entire face in an unembellished way.

OUTRAGEOUS ACTS

Every era has its hairdo badge of nonconformity, signifying the freedom of those individuals who "just say no" to the whims of fashion. Yet the wearers of radical antihairdos usually create their own "antifashion," often just as strictly codified as the mainstream styles against which they rebel.

Consider the punk rockers, with their shocking shades of pink, orange, and green hair in odd, spiky shapes glued together with contraceptive gels. The more outrageous the better, was the punker's rallying cry, their haircuts clearly intended to shock and keep people at a distance. Such outrageous styles were worn to elicit attention but also to provoke onlookers to question their own habits.

Less rebellious women may borrow from certain radical looks to make a point. Examples include the clean flattop of Grace Jones and the dreadlocks of the Rastafarians. Dreadlocks, or "fear locks," are part of the Rastafarian culture. Originally an Ethiopian style, they were adopted by Jamaican Rastas to indicate their beliefs. Unplaited and uncombed, dreadlocks bear only a slight resemblance to the neat, braided cornrows worn by African Americans and others. Often decorated with colorful beads, cornrows—which date back to 900 B.C. Africa—can transform one's head into a veritable work of art.

Shaving insignias and messages onto one's head has been popular with young men who, again, hope to shock middle-class folks and telegraph a certain message. These nineties rebels may be unaware that Catholic priests once shaved parts of their heads as a symbol of their celibacy—probably not the statement today's shaved heads wish to communicate. When a woman today shaves her head it is usually done as a social statement. Like Sinéad O'Connor, the wearer is asserting her freedom to look like the antithesis of a sex symbol.

HAIR COLOR ROOTS

How significant is hair color? In some instances, the right or wrong hair color can play an important role in a woman's career. Women in the media—the most extreme example—undergo intense scrutiny regarding their hair. *The New York Times* reported, "When Charlayne Hunter-Gault, a correspondent with *The MacNeil/Lehrer NewsHour,* recently lightened her hair, the viewer mail piled up. 'One woman said she wasn't going to listen to me anymore,' says Ms. Hunter-Gault. Another applauded her experiment with 'glamour.' Barbara Walters becomes blonder and livelier with each decade. Light hair gives her—and other former brunettes her age— a softer, more youthful look."

In this era of dark-rooted blondes, henna-enhanced brunettes, and redheaded grandmothers, none of us feels obliged to stick with our natural hair color for life. We're free to experience ourselves as a shade or two—or more—away from our authentic roots. But, for better or worse, certain hair colors tend to be associated with stereotypical personality traits: blondes have more fun, brunettes are more sultry, redheads are wild. So before making a decision to change or retain your natural hair color, let's consider carefully how different hair shades are generally perceived and how that image jibes with the look you want to project.

BLONDES

Blondes are assumed to have fun and be carefree, yet bear the stigma of being thought unintelligent and flighty. The myth of the "dumb blonde" is thought to stem from the Roaring Twenties, when flappers, considered idle and silly, bleached their hair platinum blond—confirming for many their frivolous natures. Marilyn Monroe is perhaps the quintessential blonde, and blondes often struggle to overcome the capricious, giddy, childlike image she portrayed in her films. They may feel obliged to be twice as serious to deflate such cultural myths. A blond intellectual can be doubly intimidating to men and often has a tough time putting them at ease.

Hollywood's glamorous blond pin-up girls from the 1930s—Carol Lombard, Jean Harlow, and others—were emulated by thousands of women who wanted to lift their spirits during the Depression era. And through the 1950s, Marilyn, Jayne Mansfield, and Kim Novak carried on the tradition of the blond sex kitten. The glamour of the platinum blonde faded somewhat as women became more liberated; who wanted to spend all that time on touch-ups? But the blond icon remains.

Blond hair harkens back to such classic fairy-tale characters as Cinderella, symbolic of the sweet yet passive female. Blond is the color of youth, and we may be seeking a more youthful image when we make our hair seem to be kissed by sunlight. Like sunlight, blond is devoid of evil or dark connotations. Blondes are considered innocent, especially those with curly hair. Because blond is perceived as an unaggressive color, women with blond hair tend to get away with more. Their sheen of innocence blinds others to their dark side.

The blond image varies considerably depending upon the shade. Dirty blond hair has a teasing quality to it because it mixes innocence with darkness. Its dual nature promises the best of both the brunette and the blonde. Strawberry blondes are striking because their color is so unusual and because the red highlights emote passion in the context of blond sweetness. And pale blondes are most closely associated with angelic, childlike, chaste attributes.

A glamorous blonde who downplays her image by dressing in tailored, his-for-her or subdued styles intensifies her beauty, because the contrast between the flashiness of her hair and the reservedness of her clothes is stunning. However, the playfulness of blond hair may undermine her ability to be acknowledged as a strong, competent woman.

REDHEADS

Redheads have always been considered flashy, sexy, loose, fun-loving, passionate, and slightly dangerous. Today, red hair has a newfound popularity, as growing numbers of women are attracted to the aura of vibrancy and originality it conveys.

In Greece and Italy, red hair was for centuries a prime object of desire. Witness the impact it made on the artist Titian, who gave the Venetian women in his paintings translucent, glowing red hair, the result of careful applications of soda alum and black sulfur that he allowed to sun dry.

Queen Elizabeth's hair was naturally red, as was Nell Gwynne's, the mistress of Charles II. Both helped spawn the popularity of red hair.

However, red hair has more often been regarded with suspicion. Judas was said to have had red hair, and during the sixteenth- and seventeenth-century witch-hunts, red-haired women were tortured and killed. At one time, Brahmins were not allowed to marry red-haired women. Most of the negative associations regarding red hair stem from fear, since red is the least common hair color.

Redheads are expected to be as flamboyant as their hair color. Or to be witty, mischievous, and zany, like Lucille Ball. Or volatile and devious, like Rita Hayworth. Although a lively personality doesn't necessarily accompany red hair, it is in fact a flattering color for most complexions and may cause others to respond in a more enthusiastic, open way.

DRESS CODE

Brunettes

Brunettes are generally perceived as more earthy, sophisticated, and serious than their blond or redheaded sisters. They're also believed to be more natural, since brown hair embodies the most basic of nature's colors. Darkness symbolizes complexity, and dark-haired women tend to have a certain mysterious edge. Nor is their sexual appeal in any way lacking. The filmic images of such classic brunette beauties as Sophia Loren, Elizabeth Taylor, and Vivien Leigh continue to ignite the fantasies of men worldwide. Dark hair with pale skin creates a vamplike, dramatic effect that is more striking than blond hair and light skin.

Brunettes are perceived to possess more integrity than other women since it is usually assumed they don't "lie" by dyeing their hair. And they're also seen as smarter and more complicated. In contemporary films, for example, brunettes like Sigourney Weaver are often given the intellectual roles and are portrayed as difficult to understand. Since dark colors—including dark hair—convey a greater sense of depth, brunettes usually project an image of greater intensity and substance than their lighter-haired counterparts.

Gray

When a middle-aged or older woman lets her hair go gray, it is a sign that she is comfortable enough with herself to reveal her age and who she really is. Such women project a wise, nurturing quality and an earthy stance that says they are concerned with more than just looking young. The woman who leaves her gray or white hair alone comes across as more natural and honest than the one who dyes it.

There is no pretense about gray hair. Barbara Bush's gray hair may have helped her win the confidence of the American public, since it reflected her "what you see is what you get" attitude.

Allowing yourself to be naturally gray or white actually bespeaks a certain rebelliousness, since the norm these days is for women and men to do everything they can to appear younger than they are.

MAKING A PERSONAL HAIR STATEMENT

Just as Tina Turner's wild tresses shake in tune to her gravelly music, Aretha Franklin's Afro reflects the pride in her gospel sound, Sinéad O'Connor's shaven head symbolized her honesty and irreverence, and Grace Jones's angular flattop emanates a confident androgyny; so, too, can your hairstyle convey a sense of who you are—your personality, attitude, and values.

There can be a marked psychological benefit that comes with changing your appearance, and changing your hairstyle can be a good way to jump-start a deeper change in yourself.

Whether you're breaking up with your boyfriend and need a lift, starting a new job and want to make a great first impression, or coming down with a case of the blahs and crave a fresh outlook—changing your hairstyle or hair color can work wonders. Who says personal transformation can't begin at the roots?

A HAT FOR ALL SEASONS

"When a hat is really not a hat, it's at its best."
—*Carrie Donovan*, New York Times

A flattering hat is the quintessential adornment. Hats can provide protection from the elements, express your style and creativity, reflect your status and attitude—and hide a "bad hair day."

DRESS CODE

Whether the look you're after is sophisticated, romantic, artistic, or glamorous, hats can help.

Of course, like every other garment or accessory, hats have their own meanings, depending upon style, color, fabric, and size. Large, soft, felt "hippie hats" and antique toppers convey a fanciful rebelliousness. Classic cocktail hats, on the other hand, make an impeccably correct fashion statement, elegantly finishing off a suit or cocktail dress ensemble. Obviously a hat must complement the rest of an outfit; for example, a pillbox hat would look silly with jeans and a T-shirt, just as a cowboy hat would look ridiculous atop a couture suit.

Points to Keep in Mind When Choosing a Hat

◆ The larger the hat, the more intimidating.

◆ A tailored outfit or suit changes dramatically when one dons a hat. It can add fresh spirit to a traditional suit.

◆ Consider not only the appropriateness of the hat with the outfit you're wearing, but how it frames your face, the message it sends, and if it contributes positively to your overall silhouette.

Some Hat Styles and the Personality They Suggest

◆ Cloche hats—mysterious, guarded

◆ Basque beret—unconventional, militant

- Bowler—dignified, powerful

- Frivolous hats—attention-seeking

- Boater—fun-loving

- Top hat—superior, confident, successful

- Hat with feathers—erotic

- Riding caps—charmingly upper class

- Bonnets—feminine, fun

- Veils—unattainable, intriguing

- Straw hats—down-to-earth, romantic, fun, nonthreatening

- African hats—proud of ethnic roots

WHAT'S ON YOUR MIND?

According to Jung, because the hat covers the head, it comes to symbolize what is going on inside. Wearing a new hat may therefore suggest you are altering your mind-set for that day. Depending on the style and associations, hats make us stride down the street differently: with more authority or more joie de vivre or more abandon. Hats express a wide range of moods, allowing wearers to choose how they want the world to see them.

The urge to wear a hat is the urge to improve on nature. Since hats aren't necessary, or even common these days, you are making a statement just by putting one on. You're saying there's some aspect of yourself you want to express, and you've chosen to do so by wearing something on your head.

Looking for outlets to vent our fashion creativity, we naturally gravitate toward hats. They're an accessory, but a very prominent one. Everything else about our outfit might be absolutely proper, but a hat with an imaginative flair can provide the desired spark.

Hats worn close to the face highlight our features. A hat that shapes and molds the head, embracing it rather than shielding it, is sexy—as is the wide-brim hat, with or without a veil falling seductively over the eye. Another hat with erotic overtones is the man's bowler. For over a hundred years men have worn the bowler as a sign of power and authority—the significance of which was not lost on surrealistic painter René Magritte, who featured bowlers flying through the sky in one of his most effective works. The bowler is

now a popular part of the his-clothing-for-her movement; when worn with a man's pantsuit, it lends women a look of distinction; when worn in contrast with décolletage and black lace, it can create a very erotic appeal.

A BIT OF HAT HISTORY

Hats have historically been a bellwether of social etiquette and cultural mores. At various times in history, hats have served to indicate a woman's financial means, marital status, or religion.

But beyond their overt social significance, hats have always carried a strong association with phallic power. Fashion historian James Laver believes that in times of extreme male dominance, men wear higher hats. For example, in 1850, a period heavily dominated by males, men wore tall top hats. Around 1880, when women were gaining increased freedom, the boater, a shorter hat, took the place of the stovepipe hat. And as the absolute authority of men began to weaken, they adopted the trilby—an almost feminine hat that can now be seen in Armani's women's collection.

Throughout the nineteenth century, hats were a cultural necessity; women were never seen in public without one. Up until World War I, a woman slipped on a white cap immediately upon arising, unless she was in mourning, and some type of hat or bonnet was worn every time she left the house. This changed after the war, at which point women generally donned a hat only if they were going to lunch, to conduct business, or to church. Hats were thus transformed from a social requirement to a fashion accessory.

Hats reigned in the 1930s and through the 1950s before elaborate hairdos threw them into oblivion. Although Jackie Kennedy and her pillbox hats breathed fresh air into the millinery world, hats never truly regained their prominence in the fashion world until the past decade. Now they are worn primarily to give weight to a look and visibly reinforce one aspect of the wearer's persona.

SCARVES AND VEILS

Another category altogether is headgear that flows or wraps around the head. Scarves can be perceived as either very elegant or, as in the case of the babushka, an accoutrement of economic impoverishment. Scarves became a fashionable substitute for hats in the 1960s, when Emilio Pucci splashed his with vivid banner motifs, and other designers picked up the trend. Hermès, for example, has become renowned for its equestrian prints, an unmistakable sign of prestige and financial security. A cotton scarf projects a more modest, down-to-earth message. Bandannas, for example, fall into this category.

Veils are really masks and are very important in certain cultures. Middle Eastern women shroud their heads and faces according to social and religious custom. In Western society, veils are worn by traditional brides as well as with cocktail dresses as part of a very dressy hat. If you've never had the occasion to wear a veil, you're missing out on a unique experience. Veils add to a woman's allure, sending a signal of flirtation and mystery. They conceal your identity and relieve you of the obligation to be yourself.

HAT THEMES

Hats can create a costume or finish an outfit, and it's important to know which effect you are going for. In perusing the following list of hat categories, consider what kind of message the top of your head will be transmitting.

♦ Protective hats, such as visors and headbands, create a sporty look that implies the wearer values a healthy lifestyle.

♦ Wide-brimmed straw hats have a traditionally feminine aura and suggest domesticity and provinciality.

♦ Irreverent hats project a playful, nonconformist outlook and include everything from bizarre Schiaparelli hats to whimsical straw hats that sprout fruit, vegetables, or trolls.

♦ Berets have quite a political history. They are associated with the French resistance movement of World War II, since they graced the heads of many of its soldiers. They continued to have militant connotations in the postwar period and were again made notorious by Che Guevera, the guerrilla fighter of the Cuban revolution. The classic beret has always been linked with anti-Establishment types such as artists, philosophers, intellectuals, beatniks, and revolutionaries. Today, berets are a staple in most women's wardrobes because their simple design goes so well with so many styles. (They also qualify as protective hats since they're usually made of wool and you can tuck your ears inside to keep them warm.) The essence of the beret depends upon the angle at which it is worn. Cocked to the side, it assumes a jaunty air of defiance. When pulled down straight over the head, it has a more masculine look. Seeing you in a beret, others will sense a nonconformist/intellectual aura. And wearing one may make you feel just slightly French.

◆ Masculine hats, including the aforementioned bowler, can confer an impression of authority as well as offer a striking contrast to feminine apparel. Other styles in this category include the derby, the fedora, and the top hat.

The derby, with its domed crown and turned-up brim, takes its name from the earl of Derby and is associated with the British upper class. If you wish to convey an air of privilege, the derby will do the job nicely.

The fedora has a double-edged appeal. A fedora coupled with a man's suit imbues a woman with a masculine flair. When worn with feminine clothing, it sends out ambivalent—yet enticing—signals.

And then, of course, there's the top hat. A dapper indication of material success, the top hat enlivened the evening tuxedo of the 1930s and 1940s. Worn with a man's suit, the top hat creates a timeless elegance, as when Marlene Dietrich perched a top hat atop her sexy blond head with feminine confidence and intensity.

◆ Sporty caps naturally have a relaxed air about them, as they are associated with leisure-time activities.

Cricket caps have a slightly old-fashioned association, as does the aristocratic game they're named for. Jockey caps, on the other hand, lend status to the wearer, bringing to mind socially esteemed equestrian culture. While baseball is supposed to be the sport of the masses, baseball caps have recently catapulted into the arena of status symbol. Imprinted with a coveted movie title or popular baseball logo, they're prized by both men and women. When worn backward, they can symbolize gang involvement—or at least an attitude of rebellion.

◆ Cloches hug the skull and give the impression of youth, since they are synonymous with youth movements in both the 1920s and 1960s: flappers and flower children. Because of the way they're pulled over the head, they emphasize the eyes.

◆ Cowboy hats may possibly be the most overt symbol of virility, adding height and imbuing a woman with a brawny strength. Cowboy hats allow us to live vicariously the myth of the Wild West.

◆ Hats of whimsy owe their popularity to designer Elsa Schiaparelli, who fully recognized the emphasis a hat can lend an outfit. Her whimsical "mad cap," which drew its shape from the wearer's head, became a craze after the American actress Ina Claire took a liking to it. Schiaparelli's hats were always outrageous, and women loved the way they shifted attention away from irregular or undesirable features.

Zany hats say we want to be noticed. Hats with wit and whimsy also spice up an outfit and can add a charming irreverence to tailored clothing. Beanies, soldier hats, sailor caps, berets, and cocktail hats dotted with flowers, feathers, and veils add instant costume chic. Fun hats show dramatically that we have a sense of humor and don't take ourselves—or fashion—too seriously.

◆ Power hats are an easy way to make a grand statement. Certain styles add physical height and lend a feeling of supremacy and power. Knotted turbans are a prime example; they create stature and drama, as well as throw the spotlight onto your face.

245

DRESS CODE

For Casual Wear

- Sporty cap with T-shirt or V-neck sweater and jeans

- Cowboy hat with Pendelton shirt, jeans, or denim skirt

- Wide-brimmed straw hat with long, flowing romantic dress

- Beret with turtleneck sweater and trench coat

For Afternoons/Evenings Out

- Silk scarf wrapped turbanlike and tied in a bow or knot under the chin—with silk dress

- Plainish tailored suit with whimsical fruit-rimmed sun boater

- Mannish suit with bowler hat or fedora

- Wide-brimmed, head-hugging hat with sexy décolletage dress

Index

247

INDEX

248